What I Didn't Ex
When I V
EXPECTING

Tina Trikha is a mother of three school-going children. She has lived and worked in India, Hong Kong and the United States, and presently calls Mumbai her home. She holds degrees from the Massachusetts Institute of Technology and the Wharton School of Business, and finds those particularly useful when trying to teach multiplication to her children.

What I Didn't Expect When I Was EXPECTING

TINA TRIKHA

RUPA

Published by
Rupa Publications India Pvt. Ltd 2016
7/16, Ansari Road, Daryaganj
New Delhi 110002

Sales Centres:
Allahabad Bengaluru Chennai
Hyderabad Jaipur Kathmandu
Kolkata Mumbai

Copyright © Tina Trikha 2016

The views and opinions expressed in this book are the author's own and the facts are as reported by her which have been verified to the extent possible, and the publishers are not in any way liable for the same.

All rights reserved.
No part of this publication may be reproduced, transmitted, or stored in a retrieval system, in any form or by any means, electronic, mechanical, photocopying, recording or otherwise, without the prior permission of the publisher.

ISBN: 978-81-291-3966-5

First impression 2016

10 9 8 7 6 5 4 3 2 1

The moral right of the author has been asserted.

Printed by Parksons Graphics Pvt. Ltd., India

This book is sold subject to the condition that it shall not, by way of trade or otherwise, be lent, resold, hired out, or otherwise circulated, without the publisher's prior consent, in any form of binding or cover other than that in which it is published.

*To my parents who have loved me unconditionally
and my children who have taught me how to do the same.*

Contents

Foreword   *ix*

1. What Really is Normal? — 1
2. The Start of My Journey — 6
3. Drowning in Advice — 13
4. The Bond can Take Time — 18
5. Breastfeeding is Not Easy — 24
6. The Working Mother's Guilt — 32
7. Finding the Right Nanny, and then Being Jealous of Her — 37
8. Mealtime Woes — 41
9. Feeling the Pain of Another Mother — 46
10. Infatuation with Bodily Excretions — 49
11. Teething Issues of a Different Kind — 52
12. Whose Sandbox is It, Anyway? — 57
13. When Your Spouse Becomes a Stranger — 61
14. Sleep—a Rare Luxury — 63
15. Is There Ever a Right Time for the Second Child? — 69
16. Operation 'Cookie Crumble' — 73
17. Preparing an Only Child for a Sibling — 79
18. Homeward Bound — 83
19. Missing-in-action Sex Drive — 90

20.	The Battle of the Bulge	94
21.	Realizing How Fragile It All is	99
22.	Clueless on Oscar Night	104
23.	Struggling to be Myself Again	108
24.	The Innocence of a Child	112
25.	Organizationally Challenged	118
26.	The Great Retail Gender Divide	121
27.	In Search of the Elusive Balance	124
28.	Thinking Ahead to Those Teenage Years	135
29.	Travelling with Kids	137
30.	Guilt—the Constant Companion	145
31.	Surviving the Birthday Parties	150
32.	Don't Call Her a Supermom	159
33.	My Favourite Child	162
34.	Missing the 'Old' Me	164
35.	I Hate You, Mommy!	169
36.	Missing the Embrace	174
37.	Are You a Tiger Mom?	177

Epilogue   185

Foreword

I have spent the better part of the last ten years changing soiled diapers while talking a child out of his fear of the toilet seat, sterilizing bottles while watching my children lick the kitchen floor, averting temper tantrums and unlearning and relearning multiplication. I have attempted to be a tiger mom and fallen flat on my face, managed a home that perpetually resembled a tornado zone, remained (barely) sober during children's birthday parties and tried hard to stay off 'No fly' lists.

As someone who has been on both ends of the 'Mommy Wars'—a working mother and a stay-at-home mother, I faced a tough internal struggle as I tried to strive for a balance between my children and my career by leaning in without toppling over. I learned to deal, albeit through occasional cheating, with the overbearing behaviour of alpha parents on the playground, and to ignore the avalanche of advice that poured in from well-wishers who insisted on pointing out my (many) child-rearing mistakes.

It took becoming a parent for me to experience emotions that I had never known before—the intense sadness for a stranger who had lost her child, the chest-numbing pain at leaving my child in the care of a nanny and the pangs of jealousy once I realized that he favoured her over me.

None of this was what I had expected.

During my first pregnancy, I read several books written on childbirth and parenting in an attempt to prepare myself for my new role. I registered for weekly emails that described the developmental stage of the baby in my womb in detail. I spent hours on the phone with other pregnant friends comparing notes on the number of movements we were feeling, the severity of our Braxton Hicks contractions and the increased frequency of night-time bathroom visits. My husband and I attended a birthing course at the local medical centre where we learned how to recognize the signs of true and false labour, how to breathe to achieve a higher level of focus during birthing and how to choose among the variety of options available for pain management. With the help of a life-size doll, we learned how to bathe, diaper and swaddle a baby. The certificate that we received at the end of the course was proudly displayed in our living-room.

I read articles on the benefits of breast milk and extensively researched the vitamin and nutrient content of different formula brands to determine which would be the best for any top-up feeds. During my second trimester, my husband and I spent every other weekend at baby stores agonizing over the spacing between the slats in the cribs, the relative safety features and comfort levels of infant car seats, and the ease of manoeuvrability of different strollers.

I packed my hospital bag weeks in advance and made sure that all cameras were fully charged. The car never had less than a half tank of fuel. We picked the soft cotton baby clothes, the crib with the advanced safety features, the sterilizer and the BPA-free bottles. We stocked up on diapers and had the paediatrician's number saved on speed dial.

We thought we were well prepared for the arrival of our baby.

How wrong we were!

Nobody and *nothing* had prepared us for the many non-subtle changes in our lives. We had, of course, understood that our ability to go out for a movie or dinner at a moment's notice was going to be severely hampered. We also realized that a lot of important decisions such as career progression, future relocations and home selection were now going to be influenced by a new family member.

But we didn't realize that having a baby also meant getting on an emotional roller-coaster that didn't stop, no matter how loudly we screamed. We soon found out that there were a myriad of emotions (often conflicting) that we were going to experience regularly as parents and discovered that we were completely unprepared for most of them. There was a lot of available information on what to do for diaper rashes, colicky conditions and sleep training. But there wasn't much that dealt with the many emotions that new parents, and in particular, mothers, felt.

As a new parent, you experience joy, pride, anxiety, insecurity and love, as you have never known before. You experience highs and lows that you didn't know existed. And you learn a whole lot about yourself and your spouse—some good and some not so good.

There was nothing that prepared me for how imprisoned I felt in the first several weeks of my son's life when I was always required to be around to feed, change and take care of him. I had learned about the importance and the many benefits of tummy time, but no one had told me how important having mummy's own time would be for maintaining my sanity.

I was caught completely unaware by the utter loneliness I felt in the first couple of months when I craved adult conversation just to keep myself sane. I lived in a perpetually dishevelled and sleep-deprived state and was willing to pay serious money for five uninterrupted minutes in the shower.

I was amazed by the joy I felt when my infant son started to respond to me with his smiles and gurgles. I surprised myself with the anxiety I felt even as he slept peacefully. And, I fell in love with my husband all over again while listening to him sing lullabies to our child.

I had been a fairly practical and analytical person and so I was taken aback by how emotional I had become, and shocked by my rapidly declining ability to make decisions based only on facts. And I was totally unprepared for the meltdown I had when I returned to work after maternity leave. I could barely recognize the emotionally charged woman that I had become.

I also realized that it took becoming a parent myself to fully appreciate and understand what my parents had done for me. For the first time in my life, I experienced what it felt like to love someone completely and unconditionally.

Over the last decade, I have taken on many different roles as a parent to my three children. I have taken turns being their cheerleader, coach, arbitrator, tutor, masseuse, chauffeur, friend, disciplinarian and punching bag. I have been a working mother and a stay-at-home mother. Both roles have had their challenges and their joys and both have been the right choice for me at different times. I have been a 'tiger mother', pushing my children into music classes, squash lessons and hours of math practice, and I have been a 'laid-back mother'. I have judged the parenting skills of others and I have been judged for my own, and I have realized that we all live in glass houses.

Rather importantly, I have learned that what works for one family doesn't always work for another.

I have had the opportunity to raise my children in very different cultures over the last ten years—the United States and India—and have found that as different as the environment and cultures may be, many of the parenting emotions, and the joys, anxieties and hopes that are so inextricably tied to them, are very similar.

A few years ago, I started to write down some of my experiences for couples who were expecting their first child, so that they were a little more aware of the complete life change that they were soon going to experience. My aim wasn't to provide answers to new parents as there are no cookie cutter solutions for parenting. The intent was simply to prepare them for the roller-coaster journey that they are about to embark upon.

Because every single day as a parent is a new learning. Every day brings with it an experience that I didn't expect.

And I wouldn't trade it for the world.

1: What Really is Normal?

I find it rather perplexing whenever someone asks me if I had normal deliveries.

What in the world is *normal* about an 8-pound plus human being coming out of your 'certain region' while subjecting you to a magnitude of pain that transforms you from a relatively rational person into an obscenely screaming, kicking and flailing mad woman?

What is conceivably 'normal' about lying half-naked in a room full of a dozen doctors, interns and nurses while simultaneously being jabbed with several different needles?

What is normal about being told by the doctor—in front of an audience, mind you—to push, using the same muscles you would if you were terribly constipated?

What is normal about your significant other asking you to mirror his over-exaggerated breathing gestures while you go into spasms from the unbearable pain? And is it normal to want to sock him in the face when he does that?

And when all is said and done, what is normal about grabbing a gooey creature and affixing it to your chest while the doctor repairs a third-degree tear using twenty-five stitches in the aforementioned 'certain region'?

If all of that qualifies as normal, then indeed, I did have normal deliveries.

There is nothing new about 'normal' deliveries. Women have been having babies for centuries without any of the current medical facilities at their bedside. There are stories of cultures where, when the time came, women would head into the woods with a pair of bricks to squat on and emerge a couple of hours later holding a baby in their arms. In ancient Egypt, a labouring mother would engage in belly dancing and help the baby on its way out with the gyrations of her abdominal muscles. Women of the Zuni Indian tribe wouldn't speak during their own delivery. Instead, as the baby descended into the birth canal, other women around the labouring mother would scream and moan on her behalf as if to tell her that they felt her pain. I don't know about the Zuni Indian tribe women but I prefer expressing my pain myself.

My grandmother loved telling me stories of how the stronger women of her generation would have their babies at home without any fuss, and soon after the birth, return to the kitchen to put the finishing touches on the dinner for their other six children. I have never been able to authenticate her story but I know she enjoyed narrating it just to remind me of the wimp I was for yelling for an epidural at the first sign of false labour.

There have been numerous medical advances since my grandmother's time that have made the process of childbirth much safer for both mother and baby. Fortunately, for women like me who are highly averse to any form of discomfort, the advances have also included the introduction of a bevy of options that allow the labouring mother to have better pain management during the delivery, without the support of belly gyrations or sympathetic fellow screamers.

Yes, giving birth to a baby is nothing new. It is normal and natural for women to go through childbirth.

But what is normal for womankind, as a whole, does not necessarily feel normal on an individual basis. I have yet to meet a mother who remembers her childbirth process as just a regular, normal thing. Ask any woman about the day she gave birth and she will recount the details down to the minute, experiencing many of the same emotions that she felt on that day. It doesn't matter if her child is five weeks old or twenty-five years old. She won't forget.

I clearly remember the several hours of painful labour that I experienced with my firstborn and the kindness of a nurse named Rose, who wiped the beads of sweat off my forehead and fed me ice chips while subtly cautioning my husband to remain at arms-length distance from me. I remember the chaos in the delivery room when I arrived at the hospital in the middle of a stormy winter night, fully dilated with my second child and screaming in pain. He was born less than ten minutes later and the doctor didn't even have a chance to get into his scrubs. And I remember the anticlimactic arrival of my daughter. From all early indications, she was a prime candidate for a preterm birth. Instead, she remained firmly attached to my womb and had to be coaxed out with intravenous medications after the due date.

I remember each of those deliveries clearly, along with the anxiety that I felt during them and the relief when I held my newborn baby in my arms.

It made me wonder about the process of giving birth—whether Caesarean or normal—and all the different emotions and experiences that came with it.

Are you put through all the pain and discomfort of pregnancy and childbirth because that will make the fruit of your labour (no pun intended) even sweeter? So that at the end of it all, when the baby is placed in your arms, you forget the pain that you have just endured and enjoy the reward?

Is the pride that swells in your chest as you look at your baby reflective of the emotion that you are going to feel several times over when your child takes her first faltering steps, utters her first word and brings home her first drawing from school?

Is the emotional drama of that day a preview of what is to come in the months and years ahead? A practice run for the innumerable anxious moments you will have worrying about them? A drill for late-night panic attacks when your child's forehead feels warm and his nasty cough makes you much more miserable than him?

Is your immediate instinct to wrap the baby in a blanket and draw her close to you just the beginning of your overwhelming desire to always protect her from known and unknown dangers?

Are the tears that fall freely as you hold your newborn a sign of just how emotionally fragile you are going to be in all matters relating to your child? A rehearsal for the first set of immunizations, the first day of kindergarten and the first time you have to be away from home and your child?

Is the feeling of joy that sweeps through the delivery room a prelude to the happiness and elation you are going to experience several times over as a parent to this beautiful baby that sleeps in your arms?

My mother has a favourite quote—'Once pregnant, always pregnant.' I didn't understand it at first, but now I do. The level of caring and the sense of responsibility you feel for your little ones grow along with them. You continue to worry and care about them for the rest of your life. Your happiness remains contingent on their health and happiness, your sense of calm and peace forever tied to their contentment levels.

These are all emotions that parents have had for generations. Apparently, they are all very 'normal'.

2: The Start of My Journey

It was the winter of 2002 and I was late by two days.

I had been trying to conceive for over six months and was bracing myself for another false alarm. I took the early pregnancy test and put it on the bathroom counter with the test's control window showing. A faint pink colour started to come through, but behind it, rather unmistakably, two lines were appearing.

My heart skipped a beat. I rummaged through the instruction leaflets again and compared the diagram shown on the page with my test result. It matched the positive test result.

Did I take the test correctly? Did I pee on it at the right angle?

So, I took it again. Another half hour and a litre of water later, next to the bathroom sink, I had five test windows with pairs of pink lines staring back at me.

'I think that's positive,' said my husband.

I looked at him trying to read his expression. Was he happy? Was he anxious?

I'm quite sure he was looking at my face trying to read my reaction as well.

What I didn't expect when I was expecting 7

This was something that we both wanted. So, now that we were staring at the possibility in the form of five positive pregnancy tests, why were we so nervous suddenly?

We had been married for over two years after dating for six. We both loved kids and knew we wanted children of our own. We had debated the timing several times over the last year. Should we have them sooner, while we were still relatively young, or would it be better to wait for a while, till we were more settled in our respective careers? I enjoyed my job and was driven in my career, so it did make sense to focus completely on it, without the distraction of a baby, for a few more years. It seemed logical to put in the hours, gain the experience and reach the next level in my career, when I would probably have more flexibility in my schedule.

But I had this nagging feeling about my body clock. I had time on my side, but what if that wasn't enough? What if it took months to get pregnant? What if it took years to get pregnant? What if I couldn't get pregnant? Shouldn't we start early? Then if, for one reason or another, I couldn't get pregnant, at least we could start looking at alternatives.

I knew that being a mother would make managing my career a little more complicated. But I believed, perhaps more than a little naively, that I could manage it fine. My role models were powerful, accomplished and inspiring women, who managed home and work with amazing grace and success. There was no reason I couldn't do the same, I told myself.

And how much time and energy would a small baby require in the first few years, in any case? After all, they just needed to be fed and cleaned and put to bed. There wasn't much else, right? (This question, and my lack of awareness about it, would come back to bite me in the backside repeatedly over the next several years.)

And so, there we were in a tiny New York City bathroom, with five positive pregnancy tests lying in front of us.

We held hands, giggled a little nervously and hugged.

We were going to have a baby. We were going to be parents.

We were nervous, perhaps even a little terrified, because neither of us had a clue about what we needed to do.

The first thing that we did was to schedule an appointment with a gynaecologist to confirm my pregnancy, as after five pregnancy tests we still weren't sure. After the next set of blood tests ordered by the doctor came out fine, we celebrated with apple juice. We shared the news with our parents and siblings, and while they all clinked their champagne and wine glasses, I drank some more apple juice.

Given the many risks and uncertainties inherent in the first trimester, we decided that we wouldn't rush to share the news beyond the immediate family. Hiding the fact from friends meant saying no to wine every weekend, which may have raised suspicions given my past behaviour. For a few weeks, I lied about being on antibiotics, and after that, my husband surreptitiously slipped me virgin margaritas from the bar.

What was harder to deal with was the wave of nausea that swept over me every few hours while I was at work. There were days when I spent a good chunk of the morning hugging the porcelain pot in the washroom while keeping myself on mute on a conference call on my mobile. Somehow, discussions on growth strategies always made me want to retch. Just as hard was battling the fatigue that had already started to creep in.

At my ten-week check-up, I heard my child's heartbeat for the first time. The doctor had cautioned me that it was still early in the pregnancy and that I shouldn't panic if I didn't hear it through his foetal Doppler monitor. I listened intently and heard something that sounded like the galloping of a horse. It was the most beautiful sound I had ever heard. I still couldn't feel the baby inside me, but hearing that heartbeat and seeing my doctor's smiling face reassured me that all was going well. Two weeks after that, at the scheduled ultrasound scan, my husband and I could, for the very first time, *see* our baby. In the grainy image on the ultrasound monitor, we could clearly make out the head, arms and legs of our baby. It was surreal to know that this little person was growing inside me. We beamed at each other proudly.

Once we made it past the fourteen-week mark, I started to feel much more relaxed. The statistical chances of carrying the baby to term had improved substantially. My growing belly bump was making hiding the news fairly complicated, and so, we began to tell our friends, many of whom had rather interesting reactions.

Our single friends had a bit of the 'deer in the headlights' look. It was quite clear that they were wondering what possessed us to want to switch from socializing every weekend to babysitting all the time. Some of them had been down the road before with other friends who had had babies. One of them rather blatantly told us, 'Well, it's been nice knowing you. I am probably not going to see much more of you guys for the next several years.' Ouch!

From those friends who already had babies, we received smug smiles along with the congratulatory wishes. It seemed there was something that they weren't telling us. One of them laughed out loud and cryptically said, 'Another one bites the dust!'

Our married friends who did not have kids had a very

different reaction. Their faces didn't do a good job of hiding the fear which was betrayed by their eyes. 'Are we next? Do we need to think about our body clocks? Are we even ready?' While they were happy for us, there seemed to be an odd mix of conflicting emotions within them.

It was time now to share the news at work. I told my supervisor in a serious and matter-of-fact way that I was expecting, but that it would have no impact on the quality or quantity of my work. I was still very committed and focused on my career and was sure that the pregnancy would not create any diversions. I just needed a few months off around the due date. Nothing else would change, I said. I suppose I was still thinking about pregnancy as a temporary condition and not a permanent life change. Again, a misconception that would come back to bite me repeatedly.

The person at the other end of the table nodded his head and wished me well. He falteringly mentioned that if I needed any additional support in my work, I should feel free to ask for it. I looked at him quizzically and he said no more about it. I think he was trying to figure out if I was completely clueless or if the pregnancy hormones had made me unbelievably efficient.

Putting on my no-nonsense work face, I went back to work in the project room, fighting the nausea and the exhaustion. My colleagues reacted to my news in the nicest way possible after I shared it with them. They congratulated me and seemed genuinely happy for me. But some of them also walked on eggshells around me. I think they wanted to ask me how I was feeling and what my plans were but were apprehensive about how I might react. I was making sure that I showed no change in my commitment to my work. If anything, I was trying to overcompensate. And retch less.

On the personal side, I looked forward to every single doctor visit because I got a chance to hear the baby's heartbeat again and be reassured that all was going well. My husband and I eagerly awaited the ultrasound scans as they gave us a chance to see how our little one was growing. We would spend hours looking at the printouts from the scan, wondering whom the baby's profile resembled. We debated for months on the perfect name, a task our baby made harder for us by modestly crossing its legs for the first few ultrasounds, thereby making it impossible to determine if we were having a boy or girl.

Toward the end of my second trimester, we started to think about our living space. Our one-bedroom apartment was not big enough. We needed space for the crib, stroller, play mat, high chair, changing table, sterilizer and more. It was unbelievable how many hundreds of square feet of space a three-kilogram baby would need.

We needed a larger apartment. Over several weekends, we went to scout out two-bedroom apartments in the city. The ones we loved were astronomically priced and even the ones we didn't like were significantly out of our budget.

We pored over our personal finance spreadsheet, trying to work out how we could afford a larger apartment. Once we added the cost of childcare support to our living expenses and taxes, there was just no way that we could afford a two-bedroom apartment in the city without stretching our finances to a dangerous limit.

There was only one way to do this.

We had to move to New Jersey.

We were going to be part of the 'bridge and tunnel' crowd that I had once myself mocked! I admit it—I was superficial enough to care deeply about my postal address and area code.

Now, I was going to have to eat my own words.

With one month to go until the due date, we moved to an apartment on the wrong side of the Hudson River and I tearfully said goodbye to my existing dwelling.

'Does it help that you can see Manhattan from the new apartment?' my husband asked, in a rather poor attempt to humour me.

'Did it help that I could see the bottle of wine for the last eight months but not drink it?' I replied angrily.

This kid was really beginning to cramp my style, and he wasn't even born yet!

Almost on cue, he decided to kick me hard in my ribs.

'Just you wait,' I grunted, with my teeth clenched. 'Just you wait.'

3: Drowning in Advice

Having a baby means dealing with less of a lot of things. There is less sleep, minimal quiet time for oneself, fewer evenings out as a couple and depleted savings, after the exorbitant expenditure on baby paraphernalia.

But there is one thing that there is a *lot* more of once you become a parent advice.

This is particularly true in the Indian community where everyone has an opinion and everyone feels compelled to share it with the conviction of an expert. From the moment that the pregnancy is announced or imminently visible, the floodgates of unsolicited advice open up.

'Do this', 'Don't do this', 'You really shouldn't', 'This is the best thing for the baby'—these are phrases you hear almost incessantly.

'Who is your doctor? Heavens, are you really going to let a male doctor deliver your baby? That's crazy! I will call my daughter's gynaecologist and have her see you.'

Given that a male member of the species contributed to the pregnancy in the first place, going to a male doctor for the delivery didn't seem that ridiculous. However, the concept of letting an expectant couple make their own decisions is unheard of in Indian culture. And the poor couple that may try to do it can face even more stress.

'Do you think you know more than we do? We had kids and raised them long before all those parenting books came along. Listen to us. After all, we only want what's best for you and the baby.'

You know that the last statement is absolutely true, and so, you retreat quietly and wait for the next trimester and the advice that it will bring.

There is something about a pregnant belly that makes it impossible for even complete strangers to refrain from commenting and sharing their 'wisdom'. While some of the advice may be based on scientific evidence and be focused on nutrition and the general well-being of the mother and baby, there will be much more that will leave you scratching your head.

Some of the more memorable pieces of advice that I had heard included:

'Don't turn around when you sit, or else, the baby's cord can get twisted.'

'Make sure you don't have any sex when you're pregnant. The baby can see everything, you know.' God forbid the first thing your baby sees be a home porn production.

'Avoid tea and coffee completely.' I thought that advice was for caffeine avoidance but then, the person went on to elaborate further. 'In fact, you should only have white-coloured liquids. That's the secret to having a fair-complexioned baby.' I guess genetics may as well be damned!

'You should consume a lot of butter and olive oil because that helps with labour—the baby just slips out.' If that logic were true, I might as well have some banana peels too when

I am at it.

'Make sure you see a good-looking person the first thing in the morning, so that your baby acquires their good looks.' I remember scratching my head when I heard this nugget of advice from a rather prolific advice-giver. 'Hmm, the first person I usually see is my husband,' I said. 'Whom would you suggest I sleep with instead?' She did not look pleased with my insolent reply.

One of the best ones I heard during my pregnancy was, 'Make sure you only think happy thoughts. Happy thoughts make a happy baby.' At that moment, my only thought was to strangle the person who was showering me with her unsolicited advice. But since that thought did make me deliriously happy, I figured the baby would be all right.

You naively believe that once the baby is born and the pregnant belly disappears, the avalanche of advice will stop. Turns out that if there is anything that attracts more advice than a pregnant belly, it is a new baby!

Not only does it keep pouring in, but it's also often conflicting.

'You should exclusively nurse,' from one person, and 'You should use formula as a top-up,' from another.

'You should get a nanny immediately for the extra help,' was pitted against the friendly advice of, 'Do everything for the baby yourself so that the two of you get to bond.' I didn't understand how changing soiled diapers ten times a day would help me bond with my baby, but I didn't have the energy to argue.

'You should start solids by four months,' was advice given at the same time as, 'Don't even think about starting solids until six months.'

'Make sure you sleep train your baby. Let him cry for a few days—then he'll get used to sleeping by himself,' was advice from one caring aunt. But then I also heard, 'You would have to be cruel and cold-hearted to let the baby cry in his crib. You should sleep with the baby.'

'You should make sure that you get intimate as a couple again, so that you don't grow apart.' Well, what about the baby that's co-sleeping with us, thanks to your advice?

One gentleman even told me, 'You should make the baby spend a lot of time with smart people so that he becomes smart too.' I made an immediate mental note that the baby should spend minimal time with this particular advice-giver, if indeed that was how intelligence was transferred.

'You should feed on demand.' In other words, be a lactating cow on standby at all times. Or, 'You should feed only on schedule.' And then be judged as the cruel mother who ignores her hungry baby's cries.

The never-ending and conflicting pieces of advice have the potential of driving you crazy. Not only that, they can undermine your own intuition when it comes to handling and raising your baby and make you doubt your mothering instinct.

'It's much more comfortable to feed the baby without the pillow under her, but Aunt so-and-so thought I should use it. She's had three kids. She *must* know more than me.'

Opinions come from very close quarters: mothers, mothers-in-law, sisters, sisters-in-law, aunts, uncles, grandparents, close friends and co-workers. It's much easier to ignore unsolicited advice from a stranger in the mall who feels compelled to offer her two bits on how you should be raising your baby. But how does one deal with the reams of advice from close friends and family, who only have your and the baby's well-being at heart?

When the baby is only a couple of months old, you start to receive another set of advice.

'You should start planning for your next child. You don't want too much of a gap between the kids.'

'You should take your time in having the next child. Use this time to form a strong bond with your firstborn.'

'You should go back to work after your maternity leave. Don't let there be a gap on your résumé. Or else you'll regret it.'

'You should focus exclusively on the child now. Take a break from work. You won't regret it.'

In the initial years, there can be little respite from the deluge of advice. You are likely to be engulfed by persistent and unrelenting advice round the clock from well-wishers and strangers alike. You can only hope that someone else in the family, building or neighbourhood gets pregnant soon, so that some of the advice gets deflected.

The best advice I ever got was from a fellow mom:

'Remember to smile through all the advice and opinions. Even thank the advice-giver for their care and warmth. And then, do exactly what you think is right for your baby and you. Take the advice if it works for you. If not, take it in through one ear and out the other.'

Because moms truly do know what's best for their baby. We're all wired that way. And a happy mommy does mean a happy baby.

4: The Bond can Take Time

Stories abound about the magical moment when a mother meets her baby for the very first time. Countless pages have been written in parenting books and magazines about the instantaneous bond that forms between mother and child.

Having heard and read all about that magical connection while browsing through piles of parenting books and magazines, I was eager to experience it myself with my newborn. Throughout my first pregnancy, I anxiously awaited that magical moment when I would meet my baby. When it came, it was just as I had expected.

I counted ten little toes and ten fingers. I felt his curly brown hair and his soft skin. I pulled him close to me and savoured his sweet newborn scent. I put my little finger in his palm and his fingers instinctively curled around it. He opened his eyes and I instantly fell in love with him.

It was a feeling unlike any that I had experienced before. My heart was bursting with joy, pride and love. I was enormously grateful for being blessed with a healthy newborn baby.

After a couple of hours in the delivery room, I was moved to the recovery floor for new mothers and the baby was whisked away to the infant nursery. My husband left the hospital for the night, so that I could get some rest. Physically exhausted yet emotionally elated, I lay back on the pillow and fell asleep almost instantly.

In what felt like just a few short moments, I was woken up by the baby's soft cries. The nurse had brought him into the room for his feed. She handed him over to me and left. Now, whoever said breastfeeding is natural had to have been a man because there is *nothing* natural about it. For about ten minutes, the baby and I struggled in vain to align his mouth with his food source. His soft cries were getting louder and I was starting to feel the first of many frustrations with nursing. I buzzed for the nurse and told her sheepishly that I couldn't figure out how to feed my child.

'Never mind,' she said. 'You're not the first one.' She came over to help me, held one breast and squeezed it painfully to get a few drops of colostrum (early milk) out. 'The baby needs to smell this to know where the milk is,' she explained. She brought his face in front of the droplets of milk. I could see his little nostrils flare as we guided his mouth and presto—we had a latch! That wasn't so bad, I thought, as I put my head back on the pillow and relaxed while he fed hungrily.

Forty-five minutes later, the kid was still latched on.

I buzzed the nurse again. 'Umm…how long do they keep feeding?'

'It varies based on the baby, but you should let him decide in the beginning. If he's still nursing after half an hour, let him.'

An hour after we had started, he finally pulled back in his sleep with a content look on his face.

The nurse took him back to the nursery and I lay back to sleep. It felt like I had just dozed off when someone was waking me up. The baby was crying and wanted to be fed again.

'Again? What time is it?' I asked the nurse.

'It's 3.00 a.m.—three hours after the last feed was started. So it's natural for the baby to be hungry again.'

Natural—are you kidding?

I stared incredulously at the nurse who handed him over to me. This time, she said, use the other breast. She stayed around for a few minutes to witness the comical physical contortions I was doing in order to get the baby onto the breast again and then intervened. Leaning forward, she squeezed even more painfully to get him to latch on.

Nearly an hour later when I took him back to the nursery myself, I had a suspicion that I wouldn't be getting much more sleep in the early hours of the day. Sure enough, he was back to feed in two hours.

Well, I'll just have to get used to a little less sleep, I thought. It's not that bad.

Sure. It wasn't that bad. Not until we got home two days later.

It turned out that I had seen only one part of the feeding routine while I was in the hospital. I had been spared the forty-five minutes it took him after every feed to burp. Ten minutes after the burp, he usually had an eruption in his diaper, which would soil his clothes as well. That would require a twenty-minute clean-up operation. Then, he needed to be gently patted down to sleep in a completely darkened and quiet room. Like clockwork, exactly three hours after the start of the last feed, he would be up, wailing for the next. You do the math—I had exactly twenty minutes between feed cycles. Just about enough time to throw out the dirty diaper, rinse out the soiled clothes, wipe the changing table, wash my hands and put yet another load of laundry into the machine.

I had dreamed of cuddling with my newborn, singing lullabies and enjoying his smiles and gurgles. I had imagined the two of us going on long walks with the stroller, staring blissfully into each other's eyes and relaxing in the park while watching the birds. Having leaking, painful breasts, smelling of spit-up and being in a perpetual sleep-deprived zombie state were not part of those dreams.

About three weeks after the baby's birth, I had a meltdown. A complete no-holds-barred meltdown.

My mother was visiting to help me out with the baby, and one afternoon while he took his short nap, I sat down beside her and burst into tears. The reality of new motherhood was very different from what I had expected. I was exhausted and felt that my life was spiralling out of my control.

Then I told her the part that was bothering me the most. 'Something is wrong with me, Ma. I just don't feel the connection with my baby.'

Even saying those words out loud made me feel as if I was betraying my young son. But I had to express my feelings. For days, I had felt like an external life support system for the baby—completely consumed with feeding, burping, cleaning and calming him.

One day, I glanced at one of the many parenting magazines that had replaced my pre-baby reading material on the bedside table. Staring back at me from the cover page was a new mother, resplendent in perfectly applied make-up. Her coiffed curls fell gracefully on her shoulders while a young baby slept peacefully in her arms. There were no dark circles under her eyes, her skin looked remarkably fresh and her face glowed with happiness. Her serene smile suggested to me that she had complete control over her life.

In contrast to her, I was mentally and physically tired. My hair was matted and hadn't been washed properly in days. My clothes were stained with spit-up and I couldn't remember the last time I had applied any make-up. Worse, I had this growing desire to simply run away.

I felt trapped. Had I made a huge mistake? Was I just not cut out to be a mother? Was I just too selfish and self-centred to be happy giving up my life for my own child?

My mother just looked at me and smiled.

'Ok, Ma. That doesn't help. Do you think I made a mistake? Maybe, I'm just not maternal enough. All these mothers that I read about in the magazines are just so happy and bonded with their children, and I don't feel any of that.'

My mother smiled some more. 'Don't worry. Just give it a little more time. Trust me. Once the baby starts responding, you'll feel very differently,' she said.

I wasn't sure if I should believe her, but I didn't have the luxury of engaging in an argument with her. The baby was stirring in his sleep—an indication that his royal highness would soon be awake and that I should get ready to wait on him hand, foot and breast.

The next couple of weeks went on as before and I continued to feel the same way. I tried to block out my feelings to preserve my sanity. I tried not to think about feeling trapped or out of control. I tried not to scream out in pain every time I nursed him. I tried to feel happy.

And then, a miracle happened.

When he was exactly six weeks old, I was holding him in my arms and getting ready to feed him when I saw him smiling a crooked smile at me. It wasn't one of those facial reactions that looked like a smile when he was just passing gas. This looked like a real smile.

I smiled as well, a little unsure of what to expect. His smile got wider and he gurgled back at me.

I melted.

Tears started to stream down my face, but this time, they were tears of happiness. In that one instant, I knew that we were going to be okay. The bond may not have happened immediately, but it was going to happen and it would be just as strong.

We were going to be just fine.

5: Breastfeeding is Not Easy

During the first few days and weeks post-delivery, you are constantly reminded by health care practitioners, well-meaning relatives and friends, and parenting literature that breast milk should be the sole source of sustenance for your newborn.

Everyone talks about the multitude of health benefits that breast milk provides for the baby and how it is a 'small thing' for a mother to do to ensure the best possible start for her child. (Nothing like adding a little guilt to the equation.) To push some straggler moms over the fence, the ample research on the side benefit of weight-loss is presented. And so, you find yourself perpetually attached to your baby from one of the most sensitive parts of your body.

But there is very little open discussion on how difficult and draining it is for millions of women. Even the formula feed manufacturers shy away from that conversation, lest they be burned at the stake for it.

Most of the information on the topic describes breastfeeding as incredibly natural. Personally, for me, it was as natural as undergoing a root canal without the benefit of anaesthesia.

The physical aspects alone can be quite taxing. In the first month of nursing, painful, leaky breasts will wake you up at an ungodly hour every single night. That is, of course, if your screaming infant hasn't woken you up already. You will feel like you have rocks in your breasts and your nipples will squirt milk in all directions as you struggle to get your hungry baby's mouth aligned. Your nipples will be sore, cracked and occasionally even bleed from being gnawed at ten times or more every day. And your neck will be sore from sleeping awkwardly in a sitting-up position while nursing the baby. Sound natural?

Just as hard, and sometimes even harder than the physical aspects, are the many emotional constraints that come with nursing your child.

In the beginning, you feel chained to your home because of the unpredictable nature of a newborn's feeding cycle. You may have just fed her for an hour but ten minutes later, she will decide that she needs more and will scream bloody murder if your breast is not around. You nurse her for another hour and barely have enough time to recover from that before yet another demand is made. You plot to sneak away for a quick shower when she falls asleep while nursing. You carefully use your fingertip to release her mouth's grip, and while holding your breath, gently put her down in her crib. But as you tiptoe your way out of her room, while turning blue in the face from holding your breath, she wakes up and realizes that the breast in her mouth is missing.

Wailing begins again. There goes your shower. If the baby cries because you stink, it's her problem.

You haven't slept properly for days. Your neck hurts. You smell of spit-up milk. You can barely think straight and are constantly irritable with everyone else. But you tell your exhausted self that it is a 'small thing' to do for the ultimate benefit of your child. And you count the number of days left before the baby turns six months and can start on solids.

Even if, on a rare occasion in the first few weeks, you do manage to sneak away from your infant, there are other embarrassing pitfalls. When my baby was two weeks old, I needed something from the store across the road. I took a chance and rushed across, leaving him in his grandmother's care. While I was racing through the aisles, another baby in the store began to cry. I thought nothing of it, but the hormones controlling my milk let-down reflex did. The eighteen-year-old doing his summer job at the cash register stared in amazement at my T-shirt, which was getting progressively wetter all by itself.

I learned something that day. Never leave home without breast pads.

The self-inflicted pressure to feed our babies exclusively for several months is enormous. At the hospital, after my first child was born, I received a brochure on the benefits of breastfeeding. The nutrients found in breast milk, it said, could not be duplicated and were critical for the baby's brain development and long-term immunity. Lactation consultants at the hospital highlighted the many benefits and even suggested that exclusive feeding was one of the 'easiest' ways to nourish your baby without having to worry about sterilization or cost.

Despite the many false starts with nursing that my son and I had experienced while still in the hospital, I headed home with every intention of exclusively nursing the baby for a minimum of four months, if not longer. After all, as the experts said, it was the *least* I could do for my son's future benefit.

But it was hard. I was tired of being chewed upon and

stressed about whether or not I was producing enough milk to meet my child's needs. As opposed to feeding with a bottle where I could see if he had had enough to drink, human breasts do not come with any markings. And I was fairly certain it would be much easier to sterilize bottles than sit hunched up for over half the day with either the baby or an ice pack at the bosom.

If you're a social person, nursing puts a dampener on that as well. Since my son's unpredictable feeding schedules meant I couldn't venture out much myself, friends and family were kind enough to come and visit me. It was during those visits that I began to worry that my son might be exhibiting early signs of being a social pariah. Invariably, he picked those moments to wail loudest for his feed. While I would shamelessly whip out a breast and nurse in front of my female friends, I was told by my husband to be a little coy when we had male company. So, I had to retreat into a room, where my son would insist on nursing for the better part of an hour while I listened to muffled voices and laughter coming from the living-room. Thanks to nursing, I missed out on months of salacious gossip. My son ensured that he was satiated with his feed only after the last visitor left our apartment.

When he was a little over a month old and forever hungry, I started supplementing with infant formula to keep up with his appetite. The guilt that I felt, while preparing that first bottle of formula, was tremendous. I had intended to exclusively breastfeed for four months. But I couldn't. Physically and mentally, I just needed a break. I wondered how he would react to the different taste, but he lapped up the formula. I was ashamed of myself for caving in so quickly. I had put *my* needs in front of my child's and felt horrible about it. I was too embarrassed to even confess to a close friend and fellow mom that I had given my child formula. I feared that she would think less of me as a mother.

I am enormously grateful to our paediatrician who told me at our next visit that she had been formula-fed as a baby, and in her own opinion had turned out quite fine. Her words of wisdom to me were—'Feed the baby for as long as you happily can. If you're miserable, it's not worth it for either the baby or you. You'll both be better off with formula in that case.' I followed her sage advice and continued to give him a bottle of formula at night, and we were both the happier for it. He was getting enough for him to feel full and I was getting a few extra hours of rest.

Did I feel guilty about it? I did. I was still nursing him but was bothered by the fact that I was 'cheating' and supplementing with formula. But then, as I realized later, as moms, we love to self-flagellate ourselves. If it weren't exclusive nursing, I would have found something else to feel guilty about in my new role as a mom.

Another interesting aspect to breastfeeding is the supply–demand equation. Your body will produce as much as it thinks your baby wants to consume. So, if you feed more, it produces more. If you feed less, it produces less. Taking advantage of this straightforward equation, I decided to start expressing with an electrical pump when my son was two months old, so that there was a supply built up for his day feeds when I went back to work. At first, the increase in milk supply was very welcome, and I started saving up a buffer stock in the freezer. But then, I got greedy and started using the pump more frequently and for longer periods of time, in an attempt to trick my body. Soon, I was producing enough for quadruplets.

I started to feel like a prized cow in a dairy farm, with very swollen udders, squirting milk in all directions through the day. The attempt to trick my body had backfired badly. It took a painful couple of weeks to get back down to human levels of production.

Once you're back at work, you can carry along a breast pump to use every few hours. If you're lucky enough to work in an organization that is friendly to nursing mothers, you may be able to find a small discreet room with electrical outlets and a door that locks. For everyone else, the only discreet place may be the restroom. Unfortunately, that often means that instead of an electrical pump, you need to get a hand-held pump, which will kill every muscle in your arms and hands. The books tell you that for optimal milk production while pumping, you should picture your child's angelic face to help stimulate the let-down reflex. Not very easy in a public restroom where your thoughts are constantly interrupted by flushing from the neighbouring cubicles.

When my oldest child was four months old, I developed a high fever. It was diagnosed as mastitis, a bacterial infection of the breast tissue. I was put on antibiotics to cure the infection. For a week, I had to 'pump and dump', which meant to express the milk and discard it as it couldn't be fed to the baby. Fewer things have made me as distraught as pouring breast milk down the sink. The person who coined the adage, 'don't cry over spilt milk', obviously never spilled any breast milk. Because spilling even an ounce of it can drive any lactating mother into uncontrolled hysteria.

Despite the antibiotics, within a couple of weeks the fever was back. Turned out that my son was not the only one who was being nourished by my milk, the bacteria were also growing and thriving on it. After a few more weeks of trying to cure myself of the infection and repeated fevers, I was told to stop nursing completely by my doctor.

I nursed my son for one last time that evening. While I had groaned and complained about nursing for the last several months, I was overwhelmed with emotion that day. Nursing had been our time together. It had connected us.

I got misty-eyed and even contemplated not following the doctor's recommendation to quit, when almost on cue, he decided to use his freshly cut tooth to dig into my skin. That knocked me back to reality. Perhaps it's just as well, I figured. We'll just enjoy this last feed.

I did nurse my younger two children when they were born a few years later. It was easier psychologically because I knew what to expect but it still didn't feel natural when the babies were newborn infants and not very coordinated with the latch. Fortunately, having crossed the bridge with my first child, I was far less remorseful about supplementing with formula. I was fairly convinced that with my younger children, I would nurse only till I could do so comfortably—both physically and emotionally. If that meant that I would nurse only for a week, so be it.

But the angels of lactation had the last laugh. My youngest daughter threw up every ounce of formula that I ever tried to feed her. I tried every brand and every formula that was available in the market, but to no avail. She ensured that she never kept any of it down. And so, there I was, nursing her for her entire first year.

Nursing her did get much easier once she started on solids and the frequency of milk feeds reduced. Towards the end of the day, I found myself looking forward to unwinding by nursing. The close touch, her smile when she made eye contact and her content sleeping face—were all the special, private moments that I loved.

That is, until she started biting me.

6: The Working Mother's Guilt

I always assumed I would work after having kids. I had worked hard through college and graduate school and pursued my career interests. As a woman in a largely male-dominated company, I had worked hard to prove that I deserved to be there on my own merit. I had sacrificed vacations, social outings and time with family and friends to focus on my career. I couldn't just throw all that away.

I felt fortunate to be in a place and time where I had the opportunity to have a fulfilling and successful career. Women before me had shattered the glass ceiling and laid the roadmap for others.

More than anything else, I enjoyed my work. It stimulated and challenged me and gave me an opportunity to interact with many different and interesting people. And so, when I went on maternity leave, I had every intention of returning to work.

For the first two months, that intention remained in place. In fact, there were moments when I looked forward to returning to the office, as I was craving adult company and missed the excitement and stimulation of work. I also thought it would be nice to have some control over my day again, since I seemed to have completely lost it to my newborn's feeding and sleeping schedule.

Going back to work will be fine, I had thought. The baby will be well taken care of by the nanny. I'll be able to concentrate on my work and my career while spending time with him in the evenings and on the weekends. We'll all be happy. And I still have two more months of maternity leave to give him my undivided attention.

Over the next two months, my son began to respond a lot more, and after the initial phase of uncertainty as a new parent, I began to relax and enjoy being a mom. I loved his smile when he saw my face in the morning, his gurgles as I played peek-a-boo with him, and his content, peaceful look as he slept in my arms. 'I' was clearly his favourite person in the entire world, and I loved that.

I hardly slept the week before I was going to return to work. I woke up several times each night to look at his angelic face as he slept. I rechecked my checklist for the nanny—had I remembered to share all the relevant information with her? Would she know what to do if he cried for me? Would she have enough patience with him? What if there was an emergency? Would I be able to get back to him in time? I was the only one who had ever fed him. What if he refused to take the bottle from her?

And what if he thought I had abandoned him? I was nauseated by that thought.

When daylight broke on the day I was due to return to work, I was miserable. Tears streamed down my face as I handed him over to the nanny. My legs felt like lead as I walked out of the apartment, turning around repeatedly to look at him.

I was racked with guilt as I entered the office building.

Just a few months ago, I used to enter the same building with a sense of purpose and a desire to do my best. But that day, it felt very different. I had to will myself to take the elevator up to the office because a big part of me wanted to turn around and run back home to my little boy.

At work, I proudly showed pictures of him to my colleagues. As I spoke about my son, I missed him even more. I was suddenly aware of a dull pain in my chest.

I put a framed picture of him on my desk at work, turned on my computer and tried to focus on my emails. But that dull pain in my chest wouldn't go away.

Up until becoming a mother, I had never been responsible for another person. I thought nothing of staying back late to go the extra mile or more for a project. Several hours could go by working in the office without my even realizing how late it had become. I was a workaholic and I was proud of that.

But now, everything had changed. I thought of the baby often. I looked at my watch several times during the day, wondering what he might be doing at that moment. I called home, like clockwork, every two hours to check on how much he had eaten and how well he had slept.

Every time I called, he was fine. Every evening when I got home, he was happy.

And yet, a horrible feeling in the pit of my stomach wouldn't go away.

I was still keen on pursuing my career but the extent of my desire had changed. I used to be someone who raised her hand for challenging assignments. I was happy to travel anywhere for a project. Now, I thought multiple times before taking on any new project. If it required travel outside the city, it was a non-starter. If it had tight deadlines, I would politely request not to be put on the project.

I had always believed in 'leaning in' and in pursuing my ambitions with hard work and dedication. But now, I was wobbling over, fighting to keep a precarious hold on my balance.

I was one of the first ones out of the office every evening, as I rushed to make it home in time to relieve the nanny and kiss the baby goodnight. There were evenings when he was asleep before I got home. On those days, the ache in my chest was particularly bad.

I felt guilty about leaving the office early and tried to catch up on unfinished work from home, often completing it while eating the take-out food that my husband would pick up on his way back home from work. The baby would wake us up a couple of times every night but we didn't mind it in the least, because we got to see him awake for a few minutes each time.

But it was exhausting. I was running a double shift every single day. And I was barely able to keep my head above water. I was anxious about short-changing both my roles—as a professional and, more importantly, as a mother.

Many women (and several men) who return to work after becoming a parent face this tough internal battle. One where they are torn apart between the need to pursue their professional ambitions and their desire to be the most involved parent that they can be. And quite often, we have to make choices.

It was hard for me to accept but I had to face it. I couldn't stay in the express lane of the career highway anymore. I had to slow down.

I started to explore other career alternatives. I looked for roles that wouldn't require travel and wouldn't be as demanding in terms of number of working hours. I searched for jobs that would allow me to be home with my son at a reasonable time on a daily basis, without feeling the pressure of unfinished work at the office.

I found an interesting position a few weeks later that was perfect for me. It was intellectually stimulating but didn't have the same fast pace and deadlines as my current job. It would also not have the same level of either financial benefits or career progression as my current job. It may not have been my first choice if I did not have a young child, but with my new 'normal' this was one that let me strive to find that sustainable balance between work and family.

And that was the most important thing.

7: Finding the Right Nanny, and then Being Jealous of Her

Soon after my son's birth, I started searching for a nanny. I wanted to hire someone, at least a few weeks before returning to work, so that we could work out a good transition period. Turned out, I needed all that time to find someone with whom I would be comfortable leaving my baby.

The nanny selection process was long and stressful. I interviewed over thirty nannies over the phone and probed for things such as number of years they had worked in childcare, reasons for leaving previous employers and hours that they could commit to in a new job. Behind their rehearsed answers, I tried to determine how attached they had been to the children that they had cared for in the past. While I realized that at the end of the day it was a job for them, I wanted someone who would be extremely patient and caring towards my son.

I asked about ten prospective nannies to come to our apartment for in-person interactions. About twenty minutes into each interview, I would bring the baby into the room and observe how each of them reacted to him. The ones that largely ignored his entry and focused more on the pay and vacation schedule were rejected. I also rejected a few for having extremely long nails (which I feared could inadvertently scratch him) or for being judgmental about my not nursing exclusively anymore. One of them rejected us because we were a non-vegetarian household.

I tried to listen to their intonations and read into their body language to figure out if my son would be comfortable with them. I tried to gauge the confidence and, more importantly, patience levels that they would have in dealing with a four-month-old for the better part of the day.

I finally found someone who was on the elderly side, but seemed affectionate and caring towards the baby and had considerable experience working with young kids. Her references checked out and I hired her to take care of my son during the time that I would be at work. She started two weeks before the end of my maternity leave so that my son would get a chance to gradually become accustomed to her.

I rushed home at the end of my first day back at work. I had barely coped with being away from him for ten long hours. I was worried that my little boy had been as miserable as I had been and had cried himself hoarse during my absence. As I approached the apartment, I could hear him gurgling and laughing inside. A wave of relief swept over me. We had made it through day one!

Over the course of the next few weeks, I would call often to see how he was doing at home. On several occasions, I could hear him happily babbling in the background. I patted myself on the back for having found someone who was so loving and caring towards him.

One morning a couple of months later, he woke up extremely cranky. I held him and tried to soothe him. I made sure his diaper was clean and tried to feed him. I walked him around the apartment and sang his favourite nursery rhyme. His crying, however, would just not stop.

This behaviour was unlike his usual happy self. I worried that perhaps he had a tummy ache or that something else was bothering him. My husband and I decided that we would both take the day off to take him to the paediatrician. Just then, the doorbell rang and with him still on my hip and crying bitterly, I opened the door for our nanny. As soon as he saw her, the crying stopped and he extended both arms towards her. As she held him, he hugged her and gave her a big smile.

He was crying because he wanted her.

I told a close friend about this episode and she sensed my insecurity. She consoled me by saying that the baby's reaction was a very good sign. It meant that the nanny genuinely cared for him while I was out. That was something for which I should be extremely grateful, she told me. I recognized that as well but couldn't help feeling more than a little jealous about the smiles that he gave her every morning. It bothered me that while I was holding him, he would lunge towards her and want her to hold him instead of me. It upset me that in the evenings, he looked a little sad as he waved goodbye to her.

I knew we were extremely fortunate to have a loving caregiver for my son, but I was jealous of her and of the relationship that she had with him.

What hurt just as much was missing the key milestones in his first year.

The nanny called me at work one day sounding extremely excited. He had started crawling. I was happy, but also sad at the same time. I had missed his first crawl. A few weeks before then, he had sat up for the first time and I had missed that as well.

It would have devastated me if I had missed his first steps. So, I reached an agreement with the nanny. If he did take his first steps or utter his first word when I wasn't home, I requested her to keep it to herself.

The kind woman understood. She was a mother herself.

Sometime later when my son took his 'first steps', I was there. I was thrilled to see the expression on his face as he tried to balance his body and follow a stumbling path into my open arms. Knowing (or at least believing) that I had been there for this momentous milestone was wonderful. The next morning when I told the nanny that he had taken his first few steps, true delight showed on the lovely woman's face.

And so, just like that, our arrangement continued. He continued to smile broadly every morning when the nanny walked into the house. And I continued to go to work knowing that my son was well taken care of in my absence.

8: Mealtime Woes

Blessed is she whose child eats two square meals a day. From the moment babies are born, our obsession with their nutrition and food consumption begins. At the time of discharge from the hospital, you are handed a sheet to monitor the quantity of feed they take in their first several weeks. You are asked to keep an eye on several indicators. How long did they nurse for? How many ounces did they drink, if it was from a bottle? How many wet and soiled diapers did they have?

One of the first questions asked at each of the early visits to the paediatrician is about how much your child is eating and drinking. You are encouraged to maintain a chart that plots your child's growth over a period of time. Your opinion of how well you are doing as a parent is directly related to the trajectory of your child's growth curve.

If your child slips on the growth curve at any time, you panic, even if the doctor tells you that there is no reason for concern. You eye other babies on the playground and surreptitiously count their rolls of fat and compare them with those of your child. You stress over any bit of feed that is left behind in the bottle and try to coax your little one into having it, thereby marking the start of many food-related negotiations that you will have with him.

Around the six-month mark, you get the green light from the paediatrician to start solids. An enormous amount of fanfare surrounds the introduction of the first solid meal. The baby is dressed in one of his best outfits with a matching bib and seated in a brand-new high chair. The camera is perfectly positioned as the first spoon of rice cereal ceremoniously goes into the baby's mouth. His expression changes into a grimace and the rice cereal is unceremoniously spat right back at the parent. The room rings with the laughter of friends and family who have witnessed the tasting and subsequent spit-up on the parent's face, and the images and videos of the momentous occasion are circulated with great pride.

While the first instance of this regurgitation might be funny, you will not see the humour in it when it happens multiple times a day for several months at a stretch. After a few weeks, you wizen up and convert an old scarf into a bib for yourself to save your clothes. Your reaction time improves as you learn to duck just as a new projectile of semi-chewed food flies towards your face. But as you clean up the mess in the three-foot radius around the high chair, you begin to stress about whether your child is consuming enough food and nutrients to maintain his trajectory on the growth curve.

While you can control the nutrition your children receive when still in utero, you are completely helpless against their willpower and defiance after they are born. Sometime soon after they develop a newfound sense of independence and discover the word 'No', mealtimes become a power struggle. In nearly every home I know, the child wins this fight.

Every healthy meal that is put in front of the growing toddler is met with disdain and tantrums. The only meals that are spared this treatment are those comprised of macaroni, pasta, pizza and fries. Anything remotely green in colour is shunned and relegated to the corner and occasionally pushed off its precarious perch on the edge of the plate by the baby spoon. The corners of that brand-new high chair become favourite spots for hiding vegetables and mushing peas.

The paediatrician tells you not to worry when you complain about your supremely fussy eater. She tells you to be tough and not to give in. Put a healthy plate of food before him and expect him to finish it. After all, you need to let him know that you are the boss.

You return home with new courage and re-enter the fighting arena at dinner. 'I'm going to show that little brat who the real boss is', you tell yourself, as you prepare a dinner of broccoli, beans and carrots. You put the plate in front of your little one and tell him to eat up in your most no-nonsense voice. There is a stunned silence for about five seconds as your child stares at the colourful meal. An ear-piercing scream shatters the short-lived peace. Little arms and legs move in all directions as a full-onslaught tantrum begins. You beat a hasty retreat into the kitchen and put the pasta on to boil. This round goes to your toddler.

You go back to the paediatrician with your tail tucked between your legs. She is disappointed as she expected more resilience from you. But she understands—you're not the first mother that she's seen going through this food battle and you certainly won't be the last. Since offence hasn't worked in this situation, she recommends a defensive strategy. Keep putting healthy food on the table and delicately encourage Junior to have a taste. If he doesn't want it, don't push it. But don't put the French fries on the table. 'Remember,' she tells you, 'no child in history has ever starved himself. He will come around. Just be strong.'

You follow her advice and then watch as meal after meal, your little one walks away from his dinner plate barely having eaten a morsel. You know you're trying to do this for the long-term benefit of your child, but it's hard not to worry when the same baby whose rolls of fat would spill out of your hold has now become a toddler with stick-figure arms.

The paediatrician tells you that it's just a phase and that he will grow out of it, but the emotional drama that happens at mealtimes on a daily basis is exhausting. You find yourself often breaking the rules and putting macaroni and cheese slathered with extra butter in front of your little one. You rationalize the slip by looking optimistically at the nutritional content of the food items that they do eat. Carbohydrates from the pasta, calcium from the cheese and fat from the butter, complemented with multi-vitamins disguised as jelly beans, can't be too bad. And at least, the child has a full stomach (and hopefully, a few additional grams of weight) at the end of the meal.

I've spoken with several parents to find out if they had any success in getting their little ones to eat healthily. Some managed to sneak vegetables into the pasta, but my little one picked out each one of those little pieces and arranged them in a neat pile in the corner of his plate. Some parents boiled the pasta in chicken or vegetable stock, hoping that the nutrients would be absorbed through osmosis. That recipe worked a little better for my child, but one with a more discerning nose might have rejected that too.

My children are older now and have a wider repertoire of things that they will eat, including some relatively healthy options. Nevertheless, on more days than not, their school lunch boxes come home untouched. I have learned to stress less about it. My paediatrician was correct. None of them have starved themselves (yet) and despite some meandering across the growth curve, they seem fine.

When I have met a mother who has had no problems with getting her child to eat, I have told her to count her blessings. She is truly fortunate, or perhaps, as our paediatrician said, has just managed to control the feeding routine and power struggle very well.

9: Feeling the Pain of Another Mother

During my first year of motherhood, I would frequently visit an online parent community board to see how my compatriots with babies around the same age were coping. Women from across the globe participated on the board, sharing their experiences and offering support, advice and encouragement to one another. There were a variety of discussion topics ranging from tracking developmental milestones, dealing with overbearing relatives, coping with lack of sleep and adjusting to our new roles.

Discussing topics or simply reading what other mothers had to say made me feel like I wasn't alone. In fact, many other women were going through the same phase, having the same concerns and doubts and feeling the same emotions. The support from the women on that board, who were nameless and faceless strangers known just by their usernames, was incredible.

It was on the community board that I came across Lily's story. Lily was a six-month-old who had been diagnosed with leukaemia. A fellow mother on the board shared the story and also gave a link to the family's website. I went to the website and found myself looking at a picture of a beautiful cherubic baby with a wide toothless grin. It was hard to believe that she was living in the paediatric cancer unit of a hospital. Lily's mother posted regular updates about Lily's condition and it was heartbreaking to read them. My son was nearly the same age as Lily, and while I worried about his teething issues, Lily's mother was dealing with chemotherapy rounds.

Over the next few months, Lily went through a series of treatments, blood transfusions and new trials. I checked in on the family's website every single day and sometimes, multiple times in a day. Every positive turn of events that gave a glimmer of hope for Lily's recovery had me thrilled for her and her family. Any negative news would cloud the rest of my day. Unfortunately, the sad days outnumbered the happy days.

On the day of my husband's birthday, halfway across the United States, little Lily lost her battle with cancer. She was only nine months old. Her brave mother posted the tragic news on the website and thanked everyone for their support and prayers for her little girl. Just as I did every day, I went to the website hoping for a miraculous breakthrough for this adorable baby girl whom I had never met. I went numb as I read the last post from her mother, bidding goodbye to her only child. My heart sank and the tears came streaming down.

We had made plans to celebrate my husband's birthday quietly as a family. That evening, we put our son in his stroller and walked down to a neighbourhood restaurant. As much as I tried to make it a happy family moment, I couldn't. I could not get Lily and her mother out of my mind.

My husband noticed my sombre mood and asked me about it when we got home. I had mentioned Lily's story to him before and when I told him that she had passed, he was sad for her and her family. But he couldn't understand the depth of the emotions that I was feeling. I had never met the family, didn't even know their last name and yet, I was devastated by the news.

I didn't expect him to understand. Barely a year ago, I would not have understood my emotions either. At that time, I wasn't an overly emotional person. I was able to think rationally and move on from situations that were outside my realm of control. But that was before I became a mother.

Perhaps, it was because my son was so close in age to Lily that her passing affected me so much. I thought about all the milestones that I would be celebrating with my son, which Lily's mother would not, and realized that I was also feeling very guilty. Guilty about having a healthy baby in my lap while another mother buried hers. Guilty about looking forward to my child's tomorrows while Lily's mother only had her yesterdays. Guilty about celebrating a family occasion while another family grieved for their loss.

And I was scared.

I was scared that in one fell swoop, things in my life could also change drastically. Sitting by my son's side while he slept, I worried about a twist of fate that could take him away from me. Irrational thoughts and fears engulfed me over the next several days. I worried every time he coughed or sneezed. I panicked if he fell and got even the slightest bruise. I was grateful for my healthy child, but paranoid that the situation could change for me as it had for someone else.

Over the years, my children have fallen sick on occasion and they have had bruises—both small and big. And I have realized that worrying about them has now become second nature for me. I also know that I am not the only mother that feels this way. No matter how old our children become, we will always worry about them.

It just comes with the role.

10: Infatuation with Bodily Excretions

Many meals with fellow parents will be punctuated by detailed conversations around what has been found (or not found) in their babies' diapers. How often does their baby relieve himself or herself? Is that too little or too much? How about consistency and colour? Is it usually fairly homogenous or is it a mix of colour and texture?

What is it with becoming a parent that makes people with perfectly decent table manners develop, quite literally, a potty mouth? They won't think twice about saying 'please pass the spinach' and 'our baby boy has the runs' in the same breath. And the fellow parents they are with won't wrinkle their noses in disgust either.

At home, the conversation in the morning will often be something like this:

> Mom: Did you change the baby's diaper?
> Dad: Yes. Big poop.
> Mom: That's a relief. Would you pass the milk, please? He didn't go yesterday and I was getting a little concerned.
> Dad: Well, he made up for it today. By the way, did

he eat carrots yesterday?
Mom: Yes, I made him carrot puree for his dinner. I guess his poop was a reddish hue today, huh?
Dad: It sure was. And I suppose he ate some peas too. Would you pass the butter, please?

The obsession with your baby's excretory system starts soon after you bring her home from the hospital. You will be standing next to your baby's crib looking at the peaceful, angelic face of your newborn. Suddenly, your reverie is interrupted by a low, muffled sound combined with a twitching on your baby's face, which alerts you to a new semi-solid presence in the diaper area. You look at your spouse—you have spoken about this moment for months and have organized all the tools that will be required for Operation Clean-up. You have even undergone simulation with a dummy doll. You know that you're ready for this.

You get into position and start going down the checklist that has been outlined for the change. However, unlike the simulation exercise where the dummy doll lay quiet and unmoving during the diaper change, your baby will do anything but cooperate. As you gingerly unbutton the onesie and peel off the diaper, the little one will decide that it is hungry. There will be some soft cries accompanied by the fist being shoved towards the mouth. In less than five seconds, the soft sounds will crescendo into louder and louder cries accompanied by kicks, one of which will land right in the middle of the open offending diaper.

One of you runs to get a washcloth to clean the foot before the damage spreads. With the cries getting progressively louder, you manage to somehow clean your baby's bottom and foot.

If you have a boy, he will probably choose that very instant to squirt you in your face with his pee, thereby doubling the rapidly growing scope of Operation Clean-up. By the time your mission is complete, you will be covered in all forms of refuse from your angelic baby.

After a few more such instances, any qualms or hesitation that you may have felt about discussing these matters in polite company will disappear.

I remember a discussion at a social gathering where a mother described the time her eight-month-old daughter swallowed a paper clip. She rushed her to the hospital where an X-ray showed the paper clip in the baby's stomach. They were sent home with instructions for the mother to inspect each of her daughter's diapers carefully for the next forty-eight hours. Hopefully, the paper clip would pass. If not, invasive surgery might be required. As we nibbled on fancy hors d'oeuvres, the mother described in graphic detail how she poked through every bit of dropping in the diaper until she emerged victorious with the paper clip a day and a half later. Instead of being disgusted, each parent at that gathering was completely engrossed in her tale and we congratulated her on her successful excavation exercise by clinking our wine glasses.

And so the comfort with combining cocktails and diaper tales continues, until it is unseated by an even more exciting conversation topic—toilet training!

11: Teething Issues of a Different Kind

As the only child of working parents, my oldest son's social interactions during the week were limited to those with his nanny. While she was a wonderful and caring woman, we wondered if he needed to be in a more interactive environment where he could play with other children of his age and engage in different activities.

Enrolling him in day care was not an easy decision. Keeping him at home was comfortable for him and for us. He received the nanny's undivided attention and could nap or snack whenever he desired. With day care, he would have a fairly long day at the centre and would have to adjust to a stipulated routine for nap and snack time (which we recognized may not necessarily be a bad thing). The biggest advantage of day care would be the chance for him to interact more with other children in a supervised environment.

After considerable debate, we enrolled him in the neighbourhood day care centre when he was eighteen months old. I dropped him off on a Monday morning at the adorably named 'Little Penguins' classroom, where he stared at the twelve other boys and girls, who would be his play companions during the day. If I was worried about how he was going to adjust, those concerns were quickly put to rest as he waved goodbye to me and went around exploring the different play stations in the room.

A few hours later, I received a call from the day care centre. The lady on the other end started with, 'This is not an emergency...' and I was grateful for that introduction as my heart had jumped into my mouth at the sight of the centre's number on my caller ID. I was told that I needed to come in a little earlier to pick him up as the teacher needed to discuss some 'behavioural concerns' with me.

Once I reached the centre, I heard the full story. Another boy was playing with a toy which my son wanted. Since the boy wouldn't share the toy, my son, who was clearly accustomed to getting his way, decided to bite his classmate's hand. Fortunately, the other child was fine, but this kind of behaviour was not acceptable in the classroom.

I was mortified about my son's behaviour. I silently cursed my husband for the rough-housing games that he indulged in with our son, which often involved nibbling on each other's ears.

Later that evening at home, I tried to talk to my son about biting being 'bad' and the importance of using our words rather than our teeth to communicate with others. I realized that my talk had little or no impact on my son, as I got another call at work the very next day.

He had bitten another kid. This time, it was over a crayon. In his defence, purple was his favourite colour and the other child simply wouldn't share it.

I was summoned back to the day care supervisor's office that evening. As I walked through the centre, I could feel the eyes of other parents boring into the back of my head. I was the mother of a 'serial biter'. The other parents were probably just waiting to pick up their children but my imagination was running wild. I was certain that they were whispering to each other and shaking their heads while looking at me and wondering if we would be a bad influence on the rest of the day care community.

While waiting in the supervisor's office, I wondered in fear if this would become a lifelong habit for my son. Would this be his way of dealing with all situations? If his colleagues had a project that he wanted, would he bite them for it? If his friend had a nicer tie, would he bite the tie off him? Would I have to hang my head in shame for the rest of my life because my son couldn't keep his teeth in check? Where had I gone wrong?

Years later, I would wonder how Luis Suarez's mother had dealt with his childhood days. How many bite marks did he leave in his wake as he went through day care, school, soccer camp and beyond?

The supervisor came into the office wearing a rather stern look on her face. 'We have a problem. Your son's behaviour is not entirely unusual for children who haven't been in an environment with other kids, but since it has now happened twice, we need to address it.'

I nodded blankly. I could feel the words 'Biter's mother' being branded on my forehead.

'Perhaps the day is getting too long for him,' she continued. 'We are going to suggest that you pick him up post lunch for the next two weeks. After that, we can extend the hours again and see how he does.'

She might as well have yanked the chair out from under me.

For a working mother, who is struggling to just make it

through the day without something falling apart, being told that she needs to pick up her child four hours earlier than normal is nothing short of catastrophic.

But I didn't have a choice. After all, I was the 'Biter's mother'. I spent much of that evening crying and wondering where I had gone wrong in raising my child, as my husband comforted me while also gingerly suggesting that I might be overreacting.

To add insult to injury, I had to inform my colleagues at work that I needed to leave early for the next two weeks due to teething issues at my son's day care.

'What sort of teething issues?' asked my boss, with a lot of concern.

'He seems to have a biting problem with the other kids,' I replied, while shuffling my feet.

'Oh,' he said, with a wide-eyed look of surprise on his face. I was sure that he too was judging me for the kind of mother I was. And wondering that if I couldn't control my son's bite, how would I ever be able to manage a team of adults who didn't depend on me for food and shelter? It would be a biting buffet under my supervision. Team meetings would be a free-for-all.

For the next two weeks, I picked up my son early and took him to a neighbourhood park where we sat together, ate small cheese sandwiches and watched the birds and the squirrels around the trees. I spoke to him a few more times about using his words to express his feelings, but by now, I was fairly convinced that I wasn't going to be able to break his habit.

The day he went back to his full day routine was a nerve-racking one for me. I jumped every time the phone rang. I was convinced that I was going to get a call from the day care with another biting complaint. But there was nothing.

When I picked him up that evening, his caregiver was smiling at me. 'He had a lovely day,' she said.

I was overjoyed. Could it be possible that we had broken through the habit? I called my husband and gave him the great news. Our son hadn't left his teeth marks on anyone. We were thrilled. Over the next few days, my smiling and happy toddler greeted me every evening as I arrived at the day care to pick him up. He had made many new friends and was enjoying his new routine.

A couple of weeks later, I got another call from the centre. No, he hadn't bitten anyone, said the teacher when I immediately panicked and asked it if was the 'old problem'.

'I'm afraid it's a new one,' she replied. 'He's started pulling other kids' hair.'

12: Whose Sandbox is It, Anyway?

There is something about having a child that brings out the competitive streak in every parent. A person may be fairly laid back when it comes to their own self, but when it concerns their child, their inner Olympian is invariably unleashed.

During the first year, play dates (which really are sanity savers for parents who are craving adult company) often turn into discussions around whose baby sat up earlier, crawled earlier, walked earlier, said 'mama' earlier, and more. Parents begin to keep notes, consciously or subconsciously, on how many weeks their child has taken to reach a particular milestone as compared to other children. Despite the assurances from the paediatrician that each baby reaches milestones at his or her own pace, many parents still worry if their child is behind the neighbour's child by even a single day.

As the second year begins, the conversation and implicit competition move on to identifying how your child stacks up against others of the same age group in vocabulary, number recognition, mental cognition, build and athletic prowess. Parents are constantly eyeing the progress of other children, subtly or otherwise, to see how their own child measures up.

Most of this is natural and harmless. As parents, we are

curious to see how our child's developmental pattern compares with other children of the same age. We want to make sure that our little one is growing and developing appropriately.

A few parents, though, do take it to a very different level.

For instance, there is no escaping the alpha mom on the playground. She is the one who will go on and on about how smart her two-year-old child is and how the child's intelligence is something that she and her husband marvel at constantly. She will tell you about how her child already counts up to a hundred, can write the alphabet and has taught herself how to read. In fact, she is evaluating all the programmes for gifted children in the city because it is quite clear to everyone that her child is a 'genius'.

And then she looks at you and in a sweet voice, which does little to hide her condescending intent and tone, asks what your little one can do. She nods her head as you tell her that he knows the first line of 'Twinkle Twinkle Little Star', calls the cat 'Dada' and has learnt the letter 'A', although he sometimes confuses it with 'O'. She pats you on the back and says, 'Oh, don't worry. Some kids just need more time. I am sure he will be okay.'

You stare at your child, wondering if he truly is behind. Perhaps you need to read more books to him at night, make flash cards to introduce the alphabet or talk to the paediatrician about any developmental issues. You feel guilty about not using every single minute of every single day to educate your child. You worry that your negligence is costing your child a bright future.

And what does 'he will be okay' mean? Are you condemning your child to a life of mediocrity, even before he has had a fighting chance?

Your child, meanwhile, is having a great time on the

playground, laughing with his friends, picking his nose and squealing in delight as he comes down the slide. He is having a blast being a two-year-old.

There are enough of these alpha moms on playgrounds across the world, and one day, I had had just about enough of a particularly overbearing mom who couldn't stop comparing her 'genius' child to mine. So for the next couple of weeks, I played a special bath-time game with my son. I asked him the same set of questions every single evening and repeatedly rehearsed the answers with him while he played with his little rubber duck.

When I was sure we were ready, I walked over to alpha mom on the playground and sat down on the bench near her. I waited for her to reach for the bait.

Just as I knew she would, she turned to me and in an annoying, sugary voice asked, 'So has he started picking up more things now?'

We had been preparing for this moment. 'Yes, indeed. He's been picking up some things here and there.'

'Oh, that's very nice. Does he know his vowels now?' she asked, in that condescending tone which made me want to shove a few vowel sounds down her throat.

'Well, we've discovered that he actually has an interest in things that go beyond basic learning.'

'Really! Like what?' asked alpha mom, without even bothering to disguise the sneer in her voice.

'Well, he seems to be taking an interest in current affairs and also other general knowledge facts. Oh! I know this sounds crazy, so I'll just show you what I mean.' I picked up my son from the slide and brought him over for show time.

'Sweetheart, remember the person we were talking about this morning, Nancy Pelosi. Do you know who she is?'

'Shpeaker of the House.'

Alpha mom's jaw dropped.

'And I know you've been very interested in learning about the solar system. What planet has just been removed from our solar system for being too small?'

'Plu-toe.' This one was easy, thanks to my son's favourite character on the *Mickey Mouse* show.

I had to be careful to stick to the same order of questions as we'd practised in the bathtub or my entire ploy could fall apart.

'Daddy tells me that he's been discussing some of the issues of the US economy with you. I keep forgetting the name of the Federal Reserve Governor. It's Alan something, right?'

'Green-pants,' he said, with a smile because he loved how it sounded. The name Greenspan had been too hard for him to memorize, so I had made a cue card with a picture of green pants for our bath-time practice sessions.

I observed alpha mom's shell-shocked reaction and knew it was time to deliver the knockout punch.

'Oh, and I know you've been interested in the history of numbers. Who was it that you found invented the number zero?'

'Arya-butt,' he mumbled, getting a bit tired of this game. But it was clear enough for the intended audience. Free from his mom's pincer grip, my little boy bounded back towards the slide.

Alpha mom looked positively stunned. I could hear the referee blowing his whistle and knew that I had won this round. I doubted she would challenge me to a rematch any time soon.

Before she could ask any follow-up questions and discover our little act, I moved on to speak with another, less competitive parent on the other side of the playground. From there, we could watch our kids having a great time just being themselves.

They'll *all* be okay.

13: When Your Spouse Becomes a Stranger

You think you know your spouse well. After all, you've spent years together discussing a variety of diverse topics. You know each other's opinions on political and social matters. You understand each other's preferences and you have a pulse on what inspires and motivates your other half in life. You feel fairly secure in your understanding of each other.

But then, the children come along, and suddenly, several assumptions about your spouse, which you had accepted as hard facts, are no longer valid. And you wonder how well you truly know the person who wakes up next to you every morning.

The person who you thought wasn't religious is now keen to ensure that the next generation is brought up with a good understanding of religious values and beliefs. The carefree spouse who loved skydiving and other adventure sports is now obsessively padding every edge of every piece of furniture in the home to protect your child from the tiniest scratch. The person who spoke for hours at length on how test-based learning was the biggest bane of the education system is now scouring through school websites and pamphlets to compare test scores in order to determine where to seek admission for your child.

Becoming a parent changes everything, including how well you understand your spouse and perhaps even yourself. Very often, you discover that as a couple you have very different thoughts and opinions on how you want to bring up your child.

These can range from how much television or other screen time is fine for your child, to your philosophy towards family mealtimes, to how seriously you want to practise your religious beliefs and to your approach towards education. Discussions, which used to be in the abstract before the children came along, can now be quite intense—even heated—when parents have different realizations and viewpoints.

After years of intense conversations on a variety of topics, my husband and I are now quite pleasantly surprised when we discover common ground on certain parenting decisions, no matter how small. For instance, we may have differing opinions on how strongly we want to encourage (or insist upon) a balanced and nutritious diet for our children, but we both agree that our daughter looks better in purple than in pink.

Parenting is all about celebrating those small victories. It makes the other battles easier, or at least, more manageable.

Managing to find a compromise, which both parties can happily live with, is a big part of the parenting challenge. Do you compromise by finding a middle ground on most matters, which leaves neither parent happy? Does the parent with the stronger or more articulate opinion on most matters get their way, which can lead to other festering issues? Or do you take turns giving in on different matters, depending on how strongly you or your spouse believes in them?

None of these solutions is easy and none of them is perfect. But then again, no one said parenting would be easy.

14: Sleep—a Rare Luxury

I used to be a very sound sleeper. In fact, that is probably a bit of an understatement. I was the kind of sleeper the phrase 'wild horses couldn't wake her up' was coined for. I needed three alarm clocks set at ear-piercing volumes to wake me up on a daily basis. On mornings when I had to catch an early flight, a 'friends and family' calling group was organized to rouse me from my deep slumber.

Not only was I a very deep sleeper but I also needed a lot of sleep. Eight hours of uninterrupted sleep was the minimum I needed to function normally. While some of my more adventurous friends used their vacations to explore new destinations, I went to my parents' home to sleep. My ability and desire to sleep were legendary.

And then the kids came.

I had been told that in the first few months of parenthood, sleep is highly compromised. That is yet another parenting myth.

It is not for the first few months of parenthood that your sleep suffers. It is for the first several years that it suffers!

In the first year after a baby's birth, you are subjected to inhumane levels of sleep deprivation. I remember walking like a zombie with raccoon-like eyes, thanks to the dark circles. Occasionally, I would meet a friend (a fellow raccoon-eyed mom) for a much needed coffee and to share notes on raising our young babies. During one of those coffee chats, we had a rather interesting conversation on sleep.

> Friend: I had a dream last night.
> Me: Wow! I can't remember the last time I had a dream. What did you dream about?
> Friend: I dreamt that I was asleep. It was wonderful. I could see myself deep in sleep with my eyes closed, with no other human being touching me or tugging at me or calling my name or asking me any questions. It was so quiet, peaceful and beautiful.
> Me: (sighing): I can imagine. Sounds so relaxing. What happened next?
> Friend: It was too good to last. The baby woke me up by pulling my hair.

I longed for the day when my baby would start sleeping through the night and allow me to get some rest. Turned out that 'sleeping through the night' was yet another misnomer in parenting. The baby's night (from 7.00 p.m. to 2.00 a.m.) was very different from mine. Sure, he was sleeping for seven hours and I was rather grateful for that miracle, but I wished his sleeping pattern was a little more aligned with my schedule. After all that I was doing for him, I expected a little cooperation on this from his side. So I tried pushing his bedtime back by an hour to give myself an extra hour of sleep, but it backfired. Badly. He was exhausted and cranky by 8.00 p.m., which made him wake up even more during the night. I learned my lesson and backed off. Let sleeping babies sleep when they do. It was a lot easier to deal with my crankiness than the baby's.

The quality of sleep is also compromised once you become a parent. I now sleep as soundly as a watchdog and can hear a child stirring in his or her bed two rooms away. I am capable of fetching glasses of water, looking for monsters under the bed and changing diapers in my sleep. And I know from my friends that I am not the only one. Six hours of uninterrupted sleep is an extreme luxury and it doesn't happen often with young children in the house.

Another common issue that I have heard from a lot of parents is the internal alarm set inside their children on weekends. On schooldays, I have to tug at the blankets and physically lift up my children to rouse them from their deep slumber at half past six in the morning. However, on weekends, they seem to be bounding with energy at the crack of dawn. And what better place for them to practise jumps and somersaults than on Mom and Dad's bed?

Now, we can only dream of sleeping in on weekends.

One of the crucial mistakes we made was to get a queen-size bed for our room. I would recommend to all new parents that they get either a king-size or, if they can manage it, a customized super king-size bed. Honestly, it doesn't matter whether you intend to co-sleep or not. Those little buggers will come into your bed repeatedly and at some point, you will be too exhausted to carry them back every hour. Relegated to a small corner of your own bed, you will wake up terribly cranky and sore with back and neck cramps every morning.

But, as mothers, we also become creatures of habit on discomfort. When my oldest child was two, I had to go away on a two-day business trip. It would be the first time that I would be leaving him for more than twenty-four hours. It would also be the first time in two years that I would have the entire bed to myself. I was quite excited about the latter. I called the Westin hotel in advance to ensure that they had their heavily touted 'Heavenly Bed' in the room. I couldn't wait to get to the hotel and sleep comfortably through the night.

Once we got to the hotel, I turned down the offer of checking out the nightspots in the city with my colleagues. Instead, I rushed to my room, changed into my pyjamas and jumped into the supremely comfortable bed with its plush feather pillows! 'Aah! This feels wonderful,' I said to myself. My head sank into the pillow. I shut my eyes and smiled at the thought of a blissful night's rest.

Two hours later, I was still awake.

I missed the little elbow poking me in my ribs. I missed the kicks in my stomach. I missed the little hand feeling my face, making sure that I was still lying in bed while its owner inched closer to me.

I was too comfortable to sleep.

I got up and arranged a few pillows around myself, trying to replicate the feel of a three-foot individual taking up my personal space. I finally fell asleep, but it was a far cry from the kind of sleep I had been dreaming about.

Two nights later, I got back home at midnight. My son made his way into my bed soon after. Instead of trying to carry him back to his bed, I put my arm around him. In his sleep, he snuggled up next to me and pulled up his knees to lodge them in their usual spot in between my ribcage. His fingers rested on my cheek and his face buried itself in my neck. Before I knew it, I was fast asleep.

My children are older now and one would expect that sleep patterns and behaviours would be well established. But sleep remains an intensely debated topic in our home. The most common question my husband and I hear from our kids is, 'Can we please sleep with you tonight?'

Sometimes, it's posed to us at the dinner table where the children will plead and negotiate for different beds. Sometimes, it pops up when I am tucking them in, in their *own* beds, and they're still hoping for a chance to change the sleeping arrangements.

Sometimes, we're able to enforce the 'you must sleep in your own bed' rule. But at other times, we give in to those big pleading eyes. 'But I am SO tired, Mom, and I just sleep so much better when you're next to me!' Funnily enough, as soon as I give in, they cartwheel their way over to my room showing no signs of any tiredness.

Of course, as soon as one parent is convinced, the other parent has no choice but to take their pillow to the guest bed, where another child gleefully asks to join them. It is a real life application of the game theory on many nights in our home.

I told a friend that allowing the children to sleep with us was simply a way to address one of their most basic needs. Horrified, she asked if I was encouraging an Oedipus complex. I told her that it was far more basic than that for my children. They were simply hoping that they would be able to watch a little television in my room, or chat a little longer, and break their stipulated bedtime rule.

I do have my favourite when it comes to picking a sleeping companion from amongst my children. My youngest still has her baby-soft skin, which makes cuddling with her relaxing for me as well. Her siblings have noticed that she gets more than her fair share of nights in mommy's bed and have launched several protests about that. I've tried to be more equitable, but when it comes to sacrificing comfort while sleeping, selfishness usually trumps any maternal fairness rule.

Another one of my children is like a clock hand when he sleeps, rotating on the bed at frequent intervals. As a result, over the course of the night, I will be hit with a knee, foot or elbow and frequently wake with his bottom on my face. By the morning, I am sore from the physical abuse suffered from my child's various appendages. Not surprisingly, he is the one who is picked the least by either my husband or me when it comes to sharing a bed.

But I worry about instilling a fear of rejection in him. What if our constant refusal to sleep with him causes him to have relationship issues in the future? Will he and I be in a therapist's office forty years from now and discover that his mother's refusal to hold him while he slept led him to never ask another woman to share his bed?

My husband believes I am insane for thinking that, but I worry every time I see the dejected look on my son's face after I have gently said no to him and picked one of his siblings instead. Hence, to protect his future relationships and save a tidy sum in therapy, I have decided to take a few kicks in the face and jabs in the stomach in the interim.

My sleep has suffered long enough. I don't want to lose any more of it over what might happen in the future.

15: Is There Ever a Right Time for the Second Child?

Around the time that our oldest child (and at that time, the only one) was a little over two years old, my husband asked me a rather silly question.

'When do you think we should start trying for our second child?'

I looked at him and wondered if he was completely insane. Had he been living in the same home as I had for the last two years? Had the poor man suffered a blow to the head and been afflicted with amnesia? He couldn't possibly be asking this question in a rational state of mind.

If we thought about it practically for a few seconds, the answer would be an emphatic 'Never!' We had fallen for the myth of the angelic child once. We were wiser now and knew better than to fall for that again, didn't we?

After two years of sleep deprivation, we were finally able to get five straight hours of shut-eye before our son woke us up. I could finally arrange play dates where he and his friends didn't end up biting each other, pulling each other's hair or bursting into tears in less than five minutes. Now that he had a slightly wider repertoire of things that he would eat and drink, I could take him along for errands and not have to worry about carrying a back-up to the back-up bottle of milk in case he got hungry. We weren't out of diapers, but negotiations on that front had begun and hope lingered in the distant horizon.

We were even planning to be adventurous enough to take him along with us to a fancy restaurant for dinner. Miraculously, our son was not afflicted with the two-year-old tantrum stage, which made us feel very blessed! The hardest part of raising a child seemed to be behind us. There appeared, finally, to be light at the end of the tunnel.

I thought we were making our way towards that light. Why was my poor, delirious husband suggesting that we retreat and start all over again?

My husband and I had both grown up with siblings and wanted our son to enjoy and benefit from the same bonds that we had experienced. Even before we became parents, we had spoken about having more than one child with that logic in mind.

After I grudgingly accepted that my husband's question was perhaps not as insane as it had initially seemed, we began to discuss and debate the timing in detail. Should we wait till we emerged out of the tunnel completely and then start all over again, or should we take the plunge now, while we were still familiar with the contours of the tunnel and its many open manholes?

Very soon, there was one thing that was abundantly clear to both of us.

There was never going to be a 'perfect' time to have another child.

There would *always* be something that would impede it.

It could be our son's needs at that stage, a project at work, a career move on the horizon or even other family obligations and responsibilities.

The perfect or even good time to have another child may never come. We had to decide what made the most sense for us as a family. Did we want to have another child sooner, so that the siblings would be relatively close in age, or did we want to wait for a few years until our son was over the toddler stage and possibly more independent?

There were other timing considerations as well. This included thinking about my career. How would a new baby impact it in the long term? And in the short term, how would maternity leave affect my chances for a role progression in the next year?

Then, there was childcare to think about. Our son had finally settled into his day care routine, but we would need a full-time nanny for the new baby. Could our current financial situation support that? We could wait for the financial situation to get stronger and my career to ramp up further, but then we would also be older. There could be complications in getting pregnant. And we would have a lot less energy a decade later for running around after a toddler.

The questions and debates about the timing of the baby took all the fun out of making the baby! After a few months of discussion, we decided that we would start trying for our second child and leave the rest to the Fertility Gods.

I found out that I was pregnant when my son was just a couple of months shy of his third birthday. Ironically, we also realized that sometimes when you receive one blessing, you lose another. Two days after we found out that we were having our second child, our son threw a horrible tempur tantrum in full sight of the entire neighbourhood! Turns out he was a late bloomer when it came to the 'terrible two' tantrums. But he was determined to catch up.

'Great', I thought. 'This really is perfect timing.'

Being pregnant while caring for a young child was challenging. Picking up a screaming, flailing toddler who was in the midst of a tantrum and carrying him home from the playground while trying to control the ebb and flow of nausea was a regular activity for the next several months.

Empathetic to my condition, some other mothers in the playground would occasionally help me chase down my son as he ran screaming across slides and swings. One day, a mother of two children told me that having the second child didn't mean that the amount of parenting work doubled. For a few moments, I was pleased with that information. Finally, some benefits of scale.

Then, I realized that I had misunderstood. She grabbed me by my shoulders and spun me around, so that I was looking straight into her wide eyes, and whispered ominously, 'It is going to rise exponentially, beyond anything you could have ever imagined. They are going to completely take over your life and your sanity.' She clearly wasn't joking. Her piercing stare, her words and the desperation in her voice struck a deep chord of fear in my heart.

Oh Lord, what had I done?

16: Operation 'Cookie Crumble'

One Sunday afternoon as we sipped our coffee while our three-year-old son napped, I said to my husband, 'I think he's ready.'

He raised an eyebrow as he looked at me and said, 'You remember what happened the last time, right?'

On our last trip to India, our relatives had been shocked to hear that our twenty-six-month-old son was still in diapers. In India, parents tend to get their children out of diapers much earlier, some even younger than a year old. Much before Pavlov conditioned his dogs to salivate by listening to a bell, Indian parents had conditioned their young babies to be toilet trained by holding them over sinks and whistling between their teeth.

We had a mini crisis during our visit to India when we ran out of diapers and found that the neighbourhood store didn't stock them in our son's size. The shopkeeper looked at our son, then at us, then at him again, shook his head and said, 'Too big. Shouldn't be wearing them now. He should already know.' My husband and I hung our heads in shame and left the store with our son in tow.

After calling around frantically, we found a store a few miles away that did have the larger size. That shopkeeper was only too happy to offload his excess inventory onto us. 'Please buy more,' he said. 'I ordered the bigger size by mistake. No one buys them. I'll even give you a discount.'

After returning to the US from India, I was determined to train my son. I downloaded reams of toilet training advice from the Internet, ordered a colourful toilet training seat and bought child-friendly books on the topic. We read those books with him, spent weekends watching toilet training videos together and even got a sticker chart system started to motivate my young man. But he couldn't care less. Taking a cue from advice that seemed to have worked for hundreds of parents on the Internet, I dressed him in his 'big boy' underwear in the hope that that would motivate him. A few minutes later, I found a trail of pee in the apartment, which led me to him. He was reading a book (ironically one on toilet training) while sitting in his own mess. I switched tactics and carried him to the toilet seat after every half hour while singing the annoying songs that I had heard on the videos. My son demonstrated remarkable bladder control while on the seat. But as soon as he was off it, the trail of pee would begin. I knew I was executing Pavlov's conditioning experiment erroneously, but I just couldn't figure out what I was doing wrong. After weeks of wiping, mopping, washing and cleaning, I gave up. The diaper went back on.

When I spoke to our paediatrician about my son's nonchalance towards ditching the diaper, she told me to be patient.

'How long do I have to be patient? He's two-and-a-half years old and according to my family, should have been trained over a year ago. What if he never gets trained?' I asked.

'Well,' she said, 'I have yet to come across an instance when a mother has had to move to college with her child to change diapers. It will happen. Just be patient and don't rush him.'

So I didn't. I waited patiently for several more months, changing his diapers and wiping his bottom.

'So,' said my husband, putting down his coffee cup. 'Why do you think he's ready now?'

'He's over three years old now. A lot of the other kids in his day care are out of diapers and the teachers there support the training. And with the new baby coming in less than six months, I'd much rather just have one child in diapers.'

'But, do you think *he's* ready?'

'He definitely understands it. When he needs a change, he brings me the new diaper, fresh wipes and the changing mat and lies down by himself. He even knows how to dispose of the dirty diaper when we're done. If he gets all this, he must be ready.'

'I hope you're right. I'm tired of sorting the "Cookie Monster" diapers and trading for them on the playground.'

Our son had a thing for Cookie Monster.

The diapers came in a large assorted pack with various *Sesame Street* characters in the front—Elmo, Big Bird and Cookie Monster. They were all exactly the same. But our son allowed only Cookie Monster to cover his privates.

He would sit in a dirty, stinking Cookie Monster diaper all day but he wouldn't trade it for a clean Elmo or Big Bird one. So every other weekend after buying a new box of diapers, it was my husband's job to sort them by the characters on the front. The Cookie Monster diapers were kept carefully, while he went on a trading mission with the others. Fortunately, a couple of other families in the neighbourhood with kids the same age (and still in diapers) would kindly exchange their

Cookie Monster diapers for ones with Elmo and Big Bird.

'So when does "Operation Cookie Crumble" start?' he said, with a grin.

Operation Cookie Crumble began in earnest the following week. The day care teacher was extremely supportive and asked me to send my son without diapers and in his underpants. Perhaps it was peer pressure, or perhaps his teacher was just much better at convincing and conditioning him, but he was great from the start at day care and had no accidents. At home, he had a few accidents, although they were mostly when he was asleep. We started to set the alarm for at least once in the middle of the night to carry our sleeping child to the bathroom. If we didn't, he would wake me up in dripping wet pyjamas and I would have to change sheets in the early hours of the morning.

Getting him to do the big job in the toilet, however, was next to impossible. He would plead with me every morning to put a diaper on him, so that he could hide behind the couch for privacy and relieve himself.

'This is ridiculous,' I thought. If he can use the toilet for one thing, he can use it for the other. I hid all the diapers and one morning, refused to give him one. He pleaded with me but I stood my ground. I told him that he had to use the potty like a big boy. My obstinate son didn't go that day and the same story followed the next day as well. He would use the toilet to pee but that was it.

Four days later, we were in the paediatrician's office explaining to the very amused doctor the stalemate position that we were in.

'Well, he's pretty backed up,' she said, after examining his abdomen.

'I know. He hasn't gone in four days!'

'You could just give him the diaper,' she whispered to me.

'I can't do that,' I hissed back at her. 'He'll never take anything I say seriously if I do that. I'm not giving him the diaper. I am standing my ground on this one.'

The doctor sighed. She pulled out her prescription pad and started writing. 'I'm giving you a prescription for a paediatric laxative that you can use, so that he can get a little comfortable. But this is only a one-time thing. You'll have to figure out a better way to toilet train him.'

I gratefully took the prescription from her. That afternoon with the help of a baby sitter, I pinned him down and pushed a paediatric enema into him as he screamed the house down. It was not pretty. I picked him up and seated him on the toilet seat, holding him down firmly. He sobbed and finally did what he needed to do. I sobbed too.

I may have won that battle with him but I couldn't do it anymore. I didn't want to scar him against using the bathroom for life. I reconciled myself to the situation and gave him a fresh Cookie Monster diaper every morning for his big job. I also reconciled myself to the fact that I might be the first mother in history to accompany her child to college. Hopefully, he'd pick one with nice weather.

Just as I started to browse through college brochures, there was a happy turn to the story. One morning, he didn't take the Cookie Monster diaper but simply said, 'I'm going to try,' and walked into the bathroom. I held my breath. I was too afraid to even hope. I heard a few grunts and then an exuberant, 'Mama! I did it!' I ran in and looked inside the toilet bowl. My son had done it! It was one of my proudest moments. Despite the fact that I had broken every single rule of potty training a child, he had still succeeded.

Not only did my son conquer potty training but he was also extremely helpful in encouraging his two younger siblings to get trained when it was their time. Perhaps, he wanted to spare them the scarring experience he had undergone at the hands of his mother.

The day our youngest child got out of diapers was a day of big celebration in the house. We had had at least one child in diapers at home since the birth of my oldest. It had been seven years, ten months and four days. We were now officially a diaper-free household! That evening as we contemplated going out to a restaurant to celebrate our family's milestone, my husband did some rather sobering back-of-the-envelope math. Assuming a rather conservative estimate of seven diapers a day for the last seven years, ten months and four days, our children had gone through 18,120 diapers. Given the average cost of a diaper, that was nearly nine thousand dollars that had quite literally gone down with our kids' excrement.

'That's more than a semester's tuition in college,' he said.

'That's many nice vacations,' I said.

For a few moments, there was silence as my husband and I registered that number and all that we could have done with the money.

'I think I feel sick,' I said.

Our dinner plans were immediately cancelled. We weren't flushing away any more good money on this issue.

17: Preparing an Only Child for a Sibling

The world revolved around our oldest child for the first three years of his life. Weekends, vacations and evenings were all planned based on age-appropriate fun and developmental activities for him. Meals were prepared keeping his likes and dislikes in mind. Road trips were planned around his sleep timings.

Then I got pregnant again and a sibling for him was on the way. We wondered how he would react to the situation. Since explaining a sibling's arrival to a three-year-old nearly nine months in advance would make as much sense to him as modern art typically does to me, we considered waiting for a while longer, until the arrival of the new baby was more imminent.

As the trimesters went by and my belly continued to grow, the time to prepare our son for the impending change in our family drew near. Given his princely position in our home, we knew it would be unnerving for him to share the throne with another child. We wanted him to know that his position in our hearts and lives was always going to be secure.

About three months before my due date, my husband and I sat down with him and told him that he was going to become an older brother. Much to our relief and joy, he was quite happy about it. Some of his friends from day care had younger siblings and hence, the concept was not completely foreign to him. He was excited to pick names for the baby (although he was a little disappointed when we told him that 'Goofy' was not an option) and to select the baby's clothes and toys.

Every evening when I picked him up from day care, he would ask me if the baby had arrived. He obviously hadn't connected my growing belly with the new baby. I was touched by the disappointment on his face every time I said, 'Not yet'. His excitement to meet his younger sibling was a great sign, I told myself. We had been wrong to worry about any reluctance on his part to share his royal position in our home.

The delivery day (or rather night) finally arrived and my husband shared the news with our son that he now had a younger brother. Our older boy was thrilled and could barely wait for the next day when he would be able to visit the hospital to meet the baby and me. He was given the 'big brother' honour of escorting the baby back home from the hospital by having the infant car seat placed right next to his own toddler car seat.

During the first few days, our older son was excited about having a younger brother. He stood next to the baby's crib to observe him and to talk to him. He was eager to help us in taking care of him and began making plans to teach the baby his favourite ball games, so that they could play together.

But soon, the novelty started to wear off. Babies don't do much other than sleep, cry, feed and poop. He got tired of waiting by the crib for a single reaction from his younger brother. He didn't understand why the baby cried so much. And with the way his baby brother thrashed his hands and feet in all directions while sleeping, it was pretty clear, even to a young boy, that the hand-eye coordination required for most ball games was going to be challenging.

Much more upsetting to him was the amount of time the baby was spending in my lap being fed, burped or soothed. Since I was recovering from labour, I couldn't carry my older son. Even when I wasn't taking care of the new baby, I was usually too tired to gather enough energy to play with my older boy.

That wasn't the only mistake I made. While on maternity leave, I stayed home all day with the baby and sent my older son to day care for several hours, so that he continued to maintain normalcy in his schedule. While he didn't say anything to me about it, I realized later that he would have seen the younger baby as a serious threat to his position in the family. He was being sent away while mom was spending time with the new baby.

Perhaps, we should have seen the switch in his reaction to the baby sooner. We had assumed that our older son had adjusted to the new baby's arrival. Perhaps, it was what we wanted to believe at that stage. It was easier to believe that, rather than address the simmering issue of our older son feeling resentful towards his baby brother.

About a month after the baby's birth, my older son approached me and almost pulled his younger brother out of my lap in anger. I clutched the baby and instinctively yelled at my son before seeing the expression on his face. He couldn't verbally communicate his feelings, but the tears rolling down his face and the frustration in his voice as he kept repeating, 'I want your lap,' told me how insecure he was feeling.

There was no ignoring it now. We had to address it.

I started to do what I should have done from the very beginning. I made sure that my older son's time with me was not compromised. I was still nursing but got help with the baby's other needs, so that I had time and energy to spend on my firstborn. While he still went to day care, I made sure I was the one who dropped him off and picked him up, so that we could share our special time every day. And the cuddles and kisses that we both loved so much were back.

Very soon, I started to see my big boy becoming more secure and confident in his new role in the family. He grew more patient with the baby and even started to help in bathing and changing the little fellow.

A few months later, when the baby started responding and gurgling, the delight on big brother's face was evident. He was convinced that it wouldn't be long before the training for ball games could start.

The boys are older now and have an interesting love-hate relationship. At times, they are the best of friends, and at other times, they are the worst of enemies with their hands wrapped around each other's necks. But the brotherly bond between them is undeniable. They stand up for each other and protect each other. They have inside jokes which they refuse to share with their parents.

I don't know if it will stay the same when they grow up. But for now, they seem to enjoy each other's company (for the most part), and I am enjoying watching their relationship evolve.

18: Homeward Bound

Like many other people from around the world, I had moved to the United States from my home country, India, for better opportunities in the 1990s. The United States gave me opportunities, independence, friendships and even love. It was in college that I met my husband, who had also moved from India, and romance struck in the middle of calculus class.

Over the course of the next fifteen years, we had many wonderful experiences in the US. But we did miss our families back in India. We visited them for a couple of weeks every year, but the goodbyes were always tearful and painful because we knew it would be a long time before we would see all of them again.

Being away from close family at important occasions like birthdays, festivals and weddings was difficult. Not being with our aging parents when they needed our support and presence bothered us even more. The physical distance was hard and the time difference made it even more complicated. If I wanted to share something with my parents, I couldn't just pick up the phone in the middle of the day and call them. I would have to wait until late in the evening or early the next morning, so as to not wake them up in the middle of their night.

Once the kids came along, we started to think seriously about where we wanted to raise them. We wanted our children to grow up with an understanding and knowledge of their Indian ethnicity and culture and with more frequent interactions with grandparents and extended family. We were also keenly aware that it would take a village to raise our children, and the support system in India would be far greater than what we had in the US.

But the US had been our home for a very long time. We were content with our lives. Did we really want to uproot our family and move it halfway across the world? And would it be fair on our part to take our children away from the land of opportunity that we ourselves had once sought?

After many intense discussions, we decided that we were going to move back to India. Our children were still very young and we felt it would be easier for them to adjust to a major move now as opposed to in a few more years.

With the decision made, we bid an emotional goodbye to our friends in the United States. My husband held our older son's hand and I held our younger boy in my arms as we walked through Newark's departure terminal with very mixed feelings. As the plane took off, I looked out of the window and caught one more glimpse of the beautiful city skyline. I said a silent goodbye to the country that had adopted me over the last decade and a half and given me experiences for which I would forever be grateful.

We were moving to Mumbai, the financial capital of India and a city with over eighteen million inhabitants. Its population density makes every neighbourhood feel like New York's Times Square—on New Year's Eve. Cramped with people and abuzz with activity at all times of the day and night, it is a city of constant sensory overload.

We didn't have immediate family in Mumbai, but that was where my husband's new job was located. Fortunately, we would only be a couple of hours away from our families and, rather importantly, we would be in the same time zone.

The distance of a few hours was actually ideal. Friends who had gone from one extreme to another had forewarned us. Like us, they had moved back to India after being away from their families for several years. They were now living close to or, in some cases, with their families. The Indian culture is not one that espouses personal space, particularly amongst family. As a result, many of these friends were miserable from the overdose of family affection and involvement on a regular basis.

Being a few hours away was the perfect balance. We could see our families often, be with them for important events and festivals, but also get our space.

I looked over at my family as the plane began its descent into Mumbai. My husband was showing our son the lights of the city beneath us. We were excited and looking forward to our homecoming.

Over the next few weeks we were thrilled, and also relieved, to see our children enjoying themselves in India. The joy on our parents' faces and our children's smiles as they delighted in each other's company were priceless. I saw our son giggling as he heard stories from his grandmother about the trouble his father got into when he was his age. I loved watching my son eagerly learn the rules of the game from his cricket-obsessed grandfather and I saw the happiness on my husband's parents' faces to have us with them for the Ganesh festival.

The children enjoyed being pampered by their extended family, although we had to deal with the consequences of their behaviour at home. They also had the chance to understand and observe the culture of the country on their own. Rather than picking up a few phrases of Hindi from their parents or Bollywood movies, they were able to hear, understand and gradually speak the language with other people around them. Rather than hear about Indian culture from us, they were able to observe it in practice and decide how they felt about it themselves.

While the kids welcomed the extra attention they were receiving, if there was one thing that they did not particularly enjoy, it was the cheek pinch. Indians love to display affection for young ones by pinching their cheeks. My younger boy started to hide behind me whenever we met someone new to avoid the over-effusive affection and painful cheek pinch.

There were also some other adjustments. My older son was fairly confused about the size of our extended family in India. As per customs, he was instructed to refer to all adults as either 'uncle' or 'aunty', regardless of their connection to the family. After referring to over three dozen women as 'aunty' in a single week, my son looked at me in wonder and asked, 'How many sisters do you have, mom?'

The children weren't the only ones that had to adjust to, new surroundings. After fifteen years away, my husband and I found ourselves struggling at times to readjust. There were moments when things were surely lost in translation. In one instance, when we tried to open a bank account together, the account officer inquired if we were married. When we replied in the affirmative, he looked at us and, with a straight face, asked if we had any issues. In India, 'issues' is a synonym (and a fairly apt one) for children. But we didn't remember that. My husband and I exchanged surprised glances. We had argued over something trivial on the way over, but surely, he couldn't have known that. I looked back at the bank official and said, 'Well, yes we do. In fact, we have lots of issues. But we're not sure if this is the right time and place to discuss them.'

It was now the bank official's turn to look at us quizzically.

We had another one of those situations when I hired a lovely lady to come home every week to give my husband a massage. He had a back problem and the massage was recommended by the physical therapist. However, I didn't realize that our housekeeper (yet another benefit of moving to India) was scandalized by this routine and convinced that I was running a new-age brothel by exploiting my own husband. Every weekend, I would lead the woman to a room in which my husband awaited and close the door on them. When the woman emerged from the room an hour later, I paid her and thanked her for the wonderful work she did with her hands on my husband's body.

My traumatized housekeeper was convinced that I had come under the influence of 'adulterous Western culture', but said nothing to me. I only realized what she had been thinking after she confided in my mother, who came to visit a few weeks later, and told her of the 'indecent activities' that I was running in my own home. The biggest loser in this entire episode was my father, as I had to cancel the appointment that I had made for him with the masseuse, under direct threat from my mother.

If we had any doubts about our children and us being able to adjust to the social setting in Mumbai, they were quickly put to rest. Indian neighbours, renowned for being involved in each other's lives, were a huge positive for our move. My son was eagerly welcomed by the group of children who played soccer or cricket every day in the common area of the building, and soon, he had play date invitations to the homes of his new friends. A few years later, when my husband had a minor accident and required hospitalization, our neighbours took care of our children in my absence, making sure that they were safe and healthy.

Mumbai has also taught my children to be grateful for what they have and to realize that there are others less fortunate than them. Slums, where thousands of people live in miniscule spaces, surround beautiful sea-facing bungalows with manicured terrace gardens. It is not uncommon to see a luxury Mercedes sedan stopped at a traffic signal and a woman in rags carrying a malnourished infant begging for money at its windows. That sad sight, which exemplifies the disparity that exists in Mumbai, has also made my children more empathetic to the conditions that several thousands in the city live in. It has made them appreciate what they have and sensitized them to the lives of others.

A significant benefit of the move to India was the ability to outsource several household chores. Hiring people to help with household chores is very affordable in India, as compared to the United States. Delegating laundry, cooking, cleaning and driving meant that there was that much more time for me to spend on my family or me.

However, managing the people employed was a new learning experience for me. I utilized all of my prior management knowledge with limited success. I tried positive reinforcements, feedback sessions, and even performance-linked bonus incentives. Not surprisingly, the last tool worked the best of all of them.

What with getting our shipment cleared by customs,

ensuring all utilities worked, and getting our oldest comfortable in his school, it took six months for us to get settled in our new home in Mumbai. We unpacked the last box and celebrated our official 'settling in' date with a bottle of champagne.

We toasted to our new home and to the journey that we had embarked on.

A few years after our move, we went to the Unites States for a few weeks during summer vacation. The children loved their daily walks in open, green parks. They delighted in their trips to the playground where, after a few hours of play, they could cool off with sprinklers. Even a visit to the grocery store was exciting as they stared in wonder at the variety of cereal boxes that filled an entire aisle. No day was complete without a stop at a hot dog or ice cream stand. The summer vacation was unlimited fun, play and candy all rolled together.

When we returned to Mumbai at the end of the vacation, I wondered if the children would question us on why we had relocated them from the land of hot dogs, open green spaces and sprinklers to the city of limited space and sensory overload.

I needn't have worried too much. A few days after our return, one of my children came up to me and said, 'That was a great summer, mom. But it's good to be back home.'

Home will always be the place where we, as a family, are together. And for now, our home is in Mumbai.

19: Missing-in-action Sex Drive

Spontaneity and passion don't mix with motherhood. As a mother, you're tired of others being physically dependent on you for most of the day. Between feeding, dragging the kids and their paraphernalia around town, and giving piggyback rides on demand, your body takes turns being a cow, horse and beast of burden. At the end of the day, it just wants to be left alone to recharge and get a few hours of rest before the abuse begins all over again.

The problem is that your partner, whose body has not endured the same treatment during the day, does not necessarily feel the same way. He may just want a cuddle, but you know how that always ends and you just aren't in the mood for that. Romance in the past had meant fresh flowers, phone calls for no particular reason, walks down the street with interlocked fingers, candlelit dinners and shared couch space in front of the television with a glass of wine. Women need romance to get to the next level. We can't jump into the sack for the sake of it. That's what separates us from the other, less evolved species—the men.

You try to explain to your husband that you don't feel like being romantic or intimate while smelling like sour milk and spit-up. But they don't get it. So you come up with other reasons that can't be debated. The famous 'headache' was likely conjured up by an overworked and exhausted mother to politely but firmly ward off the unwelcome and completely insensitive advances of her mate.

Of course, there are also the logistical issues with the private nature of the act. As has been earlier established, your bed becomes a communal sleeping place for all living beings in the home. While you might be able to ignore the dog or cat or even kick them off the bed, it's hard to indulge in adult behaviour in front of a sleeping toddler. How, you wonder, will you explain your actions to your child if he wakes up and sees what you are doing? And what if, despite anything child psychologists say, he remembers what he sees for the rest of his life? How will you be able to sit him down, look him in the eye and talk about abstinence when he reaches high school?

'Do you really want to complicate the process of raising kids any further?' you ask your partner.

'Uh, no,' comes the befuddled reply.

'Well, then just turn around and go to sleep.'

We were quite surprised when we discovered that I was pregnant with our third child. I had missed my cycle and for weeks was quite certain that it was due to the constant stress of running after our two young boys. A wave of eerily familiar morning sickness prompted me to take the test. I stared in shock at the two pink lines that appeared in the test window. I came out of the bathroom and told my husband. He stared back at me in disbelief.

'How?' he asked.

'I have NO idea!' I replied.

'When?'

'I have no clue.'

'But we didn't. Did we?'

Since my past sins did not qualify me for an Immaculate Conception and I had had neither the time nor the energy to cheat on my husband, we deduced that there was only one plausible and scientific explanation for how I had become pregnant. But, for some reason, neither one of us could remember how and when that happened.

Great. Not only was the act rare but it was also completely forgettable.

Worse, when I told my other mommy friends that I was pregnant, they turned on me as if I had betrayed them.

'You had sex!' one of them screamed, while pointing an accusatory finger at me. 'How could you? We had a deal. No one has sex, so the husbands can't brag about it in the locker room. Now that you've made it so clear what's happening in your home, the pressure on all the other girls to have sex is going to increase! Darn it! All I want to do is sleep! Is that so hard for the rest of you to do?'

'Well, does it help that neither of us can remember how and when it happened?' I offered sheepishly.

'Liar,' she retorted, as she stormed out of the café.

I turned towards the rest of my friends, looking for support. One of them mumbled, 'Congratulations,' but the others glared at me as if I were a traitor. I had broken the trust of the sisterhood by not keeping track of where my pants were travelling.

I felt a wave of nausea hit me. I wasn't sure if it was the pregnancy or a reaction to their hostile stares that was causing it. I was fairly certain that I would have received a much warmer reception had I announced that I was having an affair and bearing an illegitimate child. At least that would have given them fodder for gossip.

So, how long exactly does this indifference to sex and intimacy last? I posed the question to a mother with older kids. She replied that it ends once the kids leave home for college.

Something to look forward to in our retirement, I suppose.

20: The Battle of the Bulge

A big concern of expecting mothers is the weight gain during those nine months. In my experience, it doesn't matter how much you gain during your pregnancy—it's how much you can lose after the baby is born that matters. Statistical analysis will prove that those two numbers are not necessarily correlated. Someone who gains twenty kilograms may lose all the excess weight easily within a few months, while the woman who diligently watched every morsel that went into her mouth and gained only five kilograms may be fighting to get them off for a long time.

I gained eighteen, twenty and twenty-three kilograms respectively during my three pregnancies. It didn't matter how carefully I ate or how much I ate. The weight just kept adding on. My doctor initially chided me for my weight gain, but after seeing the food journal that he had instructed me to diligently maintain, realized that I was one of the chosen ones destined to gain excessive pregnancy weight. Weight gain from water retention was his kind diagnosis to make me feel better.

I managed to lose all the weight that I had gained during my second and third pregnancies within six months. However, three kilograms that I had gained during my first pregnancy never left me.

Not only have those three kilograms stayed on but they've also moved around over the years. Sometimes, they hang around in a pouch on my stomach. Sometimes, they sit on my derriere, and at other times, they settle down comfortably on my thighs or dangle off my forearms. Bottom line—they've never left.

I have tried to evict them on several occasions. I joined a gym where the trainer suggested that I work out religiously at least five times a week and reduce my carbohydrate intake drastically.

Sure, I thought. That seemed to be the right way to get back into shape. After all, no pain, no gain, or as in this case, no loss. I resolved to stick to the exercise and diet plan. I was going to alternate between cardiovascular and weight training. My well-designed meal plan would limit me to no more than 1,400 calories on a daily basis.

I organized myself for success. But what I hadn't factored in were the several traps that had been set up to make me fail.

I diligently set the alarm clock for 5.30 a.m. every weekday, to squeeze in a workout before the day's madness began. However, my willpower to hit the gym was directly related to how much sleep I managed to get the night before. And with kids who acted more like owls than humans every night, I was severely sleep deprived. So when the alarm rang, it was the snooze button that got more exercise than I did.

It also didn't help that I was routinely finishing the leftover macaroni and cheese and buttered pancakes from my children's plates. I was raised in a home where wasting food was considered sacrilege, so I felt less guilty shovelling it into my mouth rather than into the garbage bin. And of course, macaroni and cheese tastes a lot better than the steamed vegetables that the diet suggested.

About a year after my youngest child was born, I joined a gym in Mumbai. Not only had the three kilograms not left me, but they were also rapidly multiplying. Desperate times called for desperate measures and I signed up for a boot camp workout class. The instructor was the gym equivalent of a drill sergeant and barked instructions on the first day of class.

'Squat lower!'

'Kick higher!'

'Move faster!'

'Don't be so weak!'

I moved more muscles in half an hour than I had cumulatively over the last year and he still wasn't done with the class. He shouted an order for jumping jacks. I was exhausted, but didn't dare disobey him and started jumping. Around the fifteenth jump, I wondered what the wet feeling in my gym pants was. I looked down and nearly froze in horror. After three normal deliveries (and only the occasional Kegel exercise), my bladder control was not what it used to be. I was jumping in my own pee.

I was highly embarrassed and never went back to that gym again, choosing instead to work out my arms by digging a spoon into a tub of ice cream every night.

It isn't just the excess weight that is the issue. It is also the finishing on the body that changes dramatically. Thanks to stretch marks, my stomach resembles a topographic map of the Himalayas with several lines, creases and elevations. While that vision has obliterated any hope of ever wearing a bikini, the cellulose on the thighs has ruled out swimming as an activity altogether.

There are other subtle changes in body proportion, such as your hips becoming just a tad (or more) wider than what they were before you got pregnant, your abdomen becoming a little (or perhaps more than a little) looser and your arms becoming a little less toned. There are also some non-subtle changes such as your chest deflating significantly and following the laws of gravity much more rigorously. Ironically, the only part of your body that gets smaller after delivery and nursing are your breasts, and that is not always a good thing.

All these changes make those outfits that you had carefully selected because of the way they fit on your body just not that flattering anymore. The price of a wardrobe overhaul is yet another hidden cost in the process of raising children.

I now have clothes in two sizes in my closet. The first are my pre-pregnancy clothes, which I will probably never be able to squeeze into again. But I can't bring myself to discard them as that would symbolize giving up on my ambition to get back into shape. On the contrary, defying all economic logic, I continue to buy clothes in my pre-pregnancy size, in an ill-advised attempt to motivate the weight loss.

The second set comprises clothes that fit me. Although I've been wearing the same size for a few years now, I keep telling myself that they're only there temporarily until I fit once again into the clothes in the original set, which are now two full sizes smaller than my current size.

Of course, we have all come across that mom who looks spectacular in her skinny jeans barely six weeks after her fourth baby is born. We have told her how wonderful she looks in her midriff-revealing tank top while secretly wanting to tie her down and force-feed her lard. We've threatened our husbands with serious bodily harm should they ever shoot an approving look in her direction. And we've hit the gym with renewed fervour—for a week.

There will be a few genetically blessed or highly disciplined women who will get back into the same shape that they were before having their babies. For the rest of us mere mortals, baggy jeans and oversized shirts will replace those slinky black numbers in the closet. Temporarily.

21: Realizing How Fragile It All is

On his second birthday, my younger son grabbed his grandmother's medication from next to her dinner plate and swallowed it before any one of us could stop him. It was a pink, heart-shaped pill and he probably thought it was a piece of candy as he bit into and swallowed it.

I immediately dialled our paediatrician who asked for the name and potency of the medicine and told me to call him back in five minutes. Five anxious minutes later, I called him again. He had looked up the effect of the medication. The intended effect was to slow the heart rate and reduce the blood pressure. The potency of the medication was for an average adult weighing sixty kilograms. My son weighed fourteen kilograms and the effect could be much more pronounced.

None of us wanted to take any chances, and the doctor recommended that we take him to the paediatric ICU unit and have him monitored through the night. In case his heart rate or blood pressure dipped, the doctor wanted to be in a position to be able to intervene.

The first thing I did after hanging up the phone was to try to get my son to throw up the medicine. I rinsed his mouth and stuck my finger down his throat to get him to throw up.

While he seemed to have no problem throwing up after eating any bit of food on a daily basis, that was the day he wanted to keep it all in. Having failed in my attempt, we got into the car and headed to the hospital.

At the triage centre, two nurses and a doctor laid him down on the bed to monitor his heart rate and blood pressure. To my son, all the attention was just a continuation of his birthday celebrations and he grinned from ear to ear. The suction cups and tubes from the ECG machine that were being placed on his chest tickled him and he giggled as the medical team studied the readings. His blood pressure and heart rate were fortunately within normal range. I hoped that meant that he was fine and we could take him home but the doctor was concerned that the effect of the medicine could last for several hours. It would be safer to keep him under observation overnight at the hospital.

We were sent to the paediatric ICU unit. Once we got there, he had to change into a hospital gown. Up until then, he had been in his own pyjamas. Seeing him in a hospital gown was extremely hard. As a mother, you do everything to protect your children from harm, injury and illness. To see your child in the hospital and know that you could have prevented it is a horrible feeling.

Then came the worst part. The doctors wanted to put an IV line into the back of his hand, so that in the event his pressure or heartbeat dropped, they could intervene immediately and not waste time searching for a vein. While that was a rational course of action, the practical aspects of putting an IV needle into the back of a two-year-old's hand and convincing him to let it stay there are very difficult. Three nurses held his hands and legs while the doctor tried to insert the needle into the back of his hand. I put my arms around my son, who was screaming away by then. I tried to calm him down by singing his favourite songs, but he would have none of it. The doctor and nurses attempted multiple times to get the needle into his vein and even succeeded once, only to have him yank it out a minute later. His blood stained the hospital sheet. I couldn't see my child screaming anymore and pleaded tearfully with the doctor to put away the needle.

If he wouldn't let the needle stay in, we would have to take our chances. In case the monitors showed any drop in blood pressure and heart rate, it would be a race to get the IV line inserted into his vein.

Fortunately, he let the probes on his chest and the arm cuff remain, so we could get the heart rate and blood pressure readings. Around midnight, holding on tightly to my hand, he fell asleep. For the next ten hours, my husband and I took turns sitting by his bedside, our eyes glued to the readings on the monitors.

My heart ached as I looked at my little boy lying on the hospital bed with wires connected to him and a bandage on the back of his hand where he had hurt himself while yanking out the IV needle.

Hospital wards are depressing places. The paediatric unit is particularly upsetting. There was a child—no older than a year—lying in the bed next to my little boy. His head was heavily bandaged and he had a breathing tube. A little girl with excruciating pain in her abdomen was screaming and getting prepped for surgery. There were children with serious illnesses or injuries in the unit. Parents took turns sitting by their children's bedsides, holding their hands, caressing their foreheads, comforting them and singing softly to them. You could see the weary, tired eyes of those parents praying for their children. Some of the children had fallen ill, some had been born with medical conditions and a few others had been in road accidents. Mine was the only one there because we had not paid attention.

A few of the parents were talking to each other about the condition and treatment of their children. They were giving hope, support and encouragement to each other. I stared down at my feet, too ashamed to look up and make eye contact with any of the parents in the ICU.

The doctor came back to check on my son in the morning. Fourteen long hours had passed since he had ingested the medicine and fortunately, there had been no adverse reaction.

He was in the clear. We could take him home.

As he fell asleep later that night in his own pyjamas and in his own room next to his brother and just a few steps away from his sister's crib, I realized how much I had taken for granted. Their sweet smell in the evenings right after their showers, their soft curls, their smooth skin, their giggles, their jumps on the bed trying to get away from me to avoid the lotion in my hand and their peals of laughter once I caught them.

I rarely paused to smell their sweet powdery scent. I applied lotion on their bodies more as a chore than as a chance to connect physically with them. I got impatient when they jumped around the house when I needed them to get into bed. I rushed through bedtime stories. I anxiously looked at the clock while they lay in bed asking me to wait by their sides until they fell asleep.

I was going through my entire day with a 'to-do' list and a focus on completing the task at hand and moving on to the next.

There were parents who might never get a second chance to enjoy those moments with their kids. I was one of the fortunate ones. In a few years, my kids wouldn't need me to read a bedtime story to them, to tuck them in or to snuggle for a few moments with them. They may not even allow me into their rooms. Would I waste this fleeting chance to build beautiful memories for myself over a completed 'to-do' list?

Or would I change my ways to enjoy those precious moments with my children? Let them jump in the puddles rather than worry about how dirty their shoes were getting? Let them spend five extra minutes playing in the bathtub, pushing bubbles around, even if it was getting late for dinner and the bathroom was getting soaked? Let them roll down the windows in the car and sing at the top of their lungs even if other people stared? And dance in the Mumbai rains together without worrying about them catching a cold?

I made a promise to myself that evening—to try and enjoy every minute of their childhood. And then I double locked the medicine box in my closet.

22: Clueless on Oscar Night

I knew that the number of movies that we would be able to see would decrease once we had children. After all, we would no longer be able to spontaneously head to the movie theatre and catch the latest release. Each movie outing would have to be carefully planned and orchestrated with the babysitter's availability. Once you add the tangible (babysitting charges, ticket prices) and intangible (time away from the children or from your sleep) costs, you become fairly selective about the films that you watch in the theatre.

If you're the kind of person that appreciates movies that have received critical acclaim, are thought-provoking artistic works, or are high on the action gauge—watch a lot of them before the kids come along. You'll be too tired to see many movies in the first couple of years of parenthood. And after that, your children will start dictating the movies that you rent or go out to see.

The vast majority of our movie watching experience in the last few years has consisted of titles such as *Jungle Book, Kung-Fu Panda, Finding Nemo, Cars, Happy Feet, Frozen, Madagascar, Despicable Me* and *Up*, and their countless sequels. Our dinner table conversation has shifted from discussing the depths of the different characters portrayed or the historical significance of certain events highlighted in a movie to the relative 'coolness' levels of the animated characters.

While you can, of course, rent movies of your choice and watch them at home without your children, I have found that many of my parent peers don't do so. The constant interruptions from the kids who barge into your room and the frequent pauses to check on what they are doing take away from the movie watching experience.

Over time, one even stops reading the reviews of movies intended for grown-ups. After missing several movies on the 'must-see' lists of respected movie critics, it just gets too depressing.

Movie award shows, when televised, will highlight for you the number of movies that you have completely missed (in more ways than one) during the past year. You will slowly realize, as you watch the shows, that *Hurt Locker* was not a movie on sport injury rehabilitation, *Milk* was not a documentary on the risks of excessive calcification in the human body, and *No Country for Old Men* was not about the lack of available space for retirement homes. You will also learn that *Help* was not a feature depicting a cry from an overworked mother, *Gravity* was not a mother's realization that the forces of nature were now against her post-partum body, *Imitation Game* was not a story about a child mimicking others on a playground, and *12 Years A Slave* was not a story of a parent's journey through their child's school life.

Some of my childhood memories are of watching movies with my parents. These were fun weekend afternoons when we would go to the theatre together and enjoy the feature film as a family. The movies weren't necessarily kids' movies and were definitely not animated, but were entertaining and appropriate for the entire family to watch together and discuss later.

When we watched movies on video at home with my family, on the few occasions that there was something ever so slightly inappropriate (like a boy and girl holding hands with less than six inches of space between them) shown, my father would ask me to fetch him a glass of water from the kitchen. It didn't take me long to associate the water fetching chore with the (supposedly) illicit on-screen content.

Unfortunately, they just don't make family movies like they used to anymore. It's hard today to find a movie that isn't targeted solely towards kids and yet doesn't have a liberal sprinkling of sexual innuendos, inappropriate language and references to violence. More recently, I tried the water glass strategy with my pre-teen son. By the end of the first half hour of the movie, I had seven glasses of water in front of me.

Perhaps it is a reflection of the changing times that we live in, but if you want to maintain the bubble of innocence around your kids for a bit longer, you end up going to the movies considerably less and a lot more selectively. And since sending your child to fetch a glass of water while at the movie theatre is not practical, the only movies that you can see on the big screen are the children's films.

A common sight at movie theatres showing children's movies is a line of kids who are bouncing up and down and barely able to control their enthusiasm, alongside adults who are carrying popcorn bags and earplugs and wearing pained expressions. I am not sure if it is a reflection on how much better kids' movies have become or how low my bar for good cinema has fallen, but I have recently found myself recommending a few of my children's favourite movies to adults. I have received pitiful looks in response from those adults.

For better or for worse, there has been a surge in the number of children's movies released in the last few years, no doubt encouraged by the commercial success that has been supported by parents such as myself. And as if it isn't enough that we have to watch the movie first in the theatre and then multiple times on DVD, the kids also want to own the latest action figures or toys associated with the movie to relive the experience.

And relive the experience is something that they love to do. On an afternoon when I was reprimanding my sons for something naughty they had done, my daughter walked by with her Elsa doll from the Disney movie *Frozen* singing, 'Let it go. Let it go.' Obviously my sons, who were holding their sides with uncontrollable laughter, failed to get any part of my message on their inappropriate behaviour.

Airplanes are now the only places where we can watch movies that *we* want to see. Having a personal screen and headphones to see your own selection while the child in the seat next to you watches yet another animated movie is the best cinematic experience we can get. It's a bit of a step down from the in-theatre experience with the large screen and quality acoustics. Popcorn is also not included, but then again, beggars can't be choosers.

23: Struggling to be Myself Again

It started soon after the birth of my third child.

I was fine for the first few weeks after her birth, or at least as fine as any mother with three children under the age of five could be. I was tired and at times even overwhelmed, but that was normal for the phase that I was in. The novelty of having a baby in the house had not yet worn off for the boys and they enjoyed laughing at the funny expressions that their sister made in her sleep. I was grateful to have three healthy children.

But then, around the time my daughter was two months old, I started to feel anxious for no particular reason. I would get up in the middle of the night, even while she slept, to check on her breathing. Then I would check on her brothers to make sure that they were both fine. Despite being tired, I couldn't fall asleep. I would imagine that my children were calling out to me and I would often run into their rooms at night in a state of near panic.

I started to worry incessantly about the three of them, particularly the baby. I worried about their safety and health. I worried about their food intake. I worried about their physical and mental development. I worried all the time.

As someone not naturally driven to such intense worry, this was strange not just for me but also for my family.

Besides feeling anxious and worried, I also felt an inexplicable emptiness. I would sit in my room and cry for hours on end for no reason. My husband would comfort me and try to understand why I was feeling the emotions that I was. I had no rational explanation. I had no plausible reason for my anxiety and sadness. And yet, the feelings of emptiness and despair wouldn't go away.

I wanted to shake them off. I wanted to pull myself out of this state and be happy again. But I couldn't. On the contrary, I seemed to be slipping further and further into a deep emotional abyss.

When I met friends, I pretended I was fine. I managed to put on a smile and engage as best as I could. A few of my friends noticed that something was amiss and asked me if I was fine. I lied and told them it was just exhaustion from taking care of the kids. One evening, when my daughter was four months old, I went to a social event, but ended up spending much of my time in the restaurant's washroom sobbing, because I couldn't control the overwhelming feeling of sadness within myself.

No one, other than my husband, knew what I was going through. I didn't want to tell my parents because they would worry. I didn't want to talk to anyone because I was confused and even ashamed of the emotions that I was feeling. I was incredibly fortunate to have a loving family with three healthy children. I felt guilty about not being content and happy.

That was a big mistake on my part. I should have reached out for help. I was going head-first into a horrible vicious cycle.

Our nanny in Mumbai helped me take care of the children

during the day. But I was not the involved mother that I wanted to be. Instead of spending time with my baby daughter and young sons, I often retreated into my room where I would keep the blinds drawn through the day.

I started to avoid people. If someone called me, I made excuses. I used to enjoy a chat over coffee with friends, but now I declined their invitations to meet. After a while, I avoided answering my phone. I didn't want to keep pretending in front of others and I was not ready to share how I was truly feeling.

My sense of self-esteem crashed during that period. I felt insecure and incompetent. Taking care of the children was my only job at that time and I was failing miserably at that. I would try to distract myself by giving myself something productive to do. I would start to organize a closet, pull out all the clothes and lay them on the bed, and then, feeling overwhelmed by the task, give up, leaving the room in a complete state of disarray, which would make me feel even more incompetent.

I was irritable and snapped at my husband all the time. Looking back, that was probably the most stressful phase in our relationship as he bore the brunt of my mood swings and anxiety. Every evening when he came home from work, he probably dreaded the chaos and gloom that he would be walking into. There were times when he would return in the evening and I would still not have had showered. I would be in a dishevelled state, wearing my nightgown, holding one crying child while another clung to my leg. I would hand the child on my hip over to him and, without a single word, walk off into my room, closing the door behind me.

I was miserable and was making my family miserable as well.

I hadn't experienced this with either of my earlier

deliveries, but I did recognize that I was suffering from post-partum hormonal changes which were impacting my state of mind. I also knew that the condition was treatable. Yet, almost incomprehensibly, I did not seek help. I still don't know why I didn't. Looking back, I wish I had. I learned later that post-partum depression affects as many as one out of every seven mothers, and hormonal imbalances that impact emotional well-being affect many more.

I did manage to pull myself out of it finally, but it took six long months. I was fortunate because I have since learned that for many women, symptoms associated with post-partum hormonal changes can last much longer and grow in severity, particularly if untreated.

It took a tremendous amount of willpower and the support of my husband for me to emerge from my abyss. I took baby steps by forcing myself to sign up for a yoga class, or taking one of my children out for a walk in the neighbourhood park. Those small steps allowed me to slowly get back to normalcy. I also allowed myself to feel empathy for myself. I wasn't myself and I was entitled to feeling a little low at times. I needed to give myself that permission.

I didn't wake up one morning to bright sunshine and newfound happiness, but the little steps helped. Some days were good and some days were not. When my daughter was eight months old, I was feeling more like my old self. And I could finally enjoy my family.

I do wish that I had sought help. One of my biggest regrets will always be those six months when I missed being completely present in my children's lives. Those were the dark months when I was there with them, and yet, I really wasn't.

24: The Innocence of a Child

26 November 2008 was a day like any other in Mumbai.

After a warm October, the weather had finally become cooler and the evenings had started to become rather pleasant. I had gone down to the play area in our apartment building with my sons while my baby daughter took a nap in the early evening. A few kids were enjoying a game of soccer in the light sea breeze. My older son joined them in their game while my younger one chose to observe it from my lap.

It was just like any other evening.

An hour later, we came up to the apartment for dinner and baths. A cricket match between India and England was being telecast live and after putting the kids to bed, I watched the last few overs while waiting for my husband to come back from work. I was about to turn off the television at the end of the match when a breaking news blurb at the bottom of the screen caught my eye. 'Explosions heard outside South Mumbai restaurant,' it said.

I flipped through a few news networks but there wasn't much more information for several minutes. One of the networks assumed that the noise was from the fireworks celebrating India's victory over England in the cricket match.

Then the news reporters confirmed that gunshots had been

fired outside a popular tourist restaurant in South Mumbai. My husband was home by then and we speculated that a street argument among a few people had probably taken a wrong turn.

A few minutes later, as we watched the news in horror, reports of gunshots at several other locations started coming through. It was becoming extremely clear that this wasn't an isolated incident of violence but something much more sinister—a carefully orchestrated act of terrorism.

This was Mumbai's 9/11.

Over the next couple of hours, we called a few friends who we feared might have been in the affected area and were relieved to hear that they were all home and safe. Everyone was shaken up by the news of the attack.

A few hours later, the siege on two hotels and a Chabad house in Mumbai continued. My husband and I finally went to bed around 2.00 a.m., expecting that it would be over when we woke up.

Early the next morning, when we turned on the television, we were shocked to see that the stand-off hadn't ended. Schools were shut for the day. Gunshots continued to ring out in those three locations. Innocent citizens were still trapped inside those buildings with worried family members desperately holding on to hope for their safety.

For the next two days, we remained glued to the television, watching and waiting for the horror that had gripped the city to come to an end. Nearly forty-eight hours after the start of the ordeal, the police announced that they had regained control of all the buildings that the terrorists had attacked. The traumatized city heaved a collective sigh of relief.

Then began the task of finding the still missing and

identifying those who had fallen to the bullets.

A few hours later, I was feeding my daughter when I heard my husband cry out, 'Oh my God!' while reading his emails. I looked across to where he was sitting and saw him holding his head in his hands.

I asked him what happened but already knew there could only be one kind of news at such a time. He read out an email which he had just received from the principal of our son's school.

One of our son's close friends in kindergarten had lost both his parents in the attack.

Just like us, they were a couple with three young children. They had probably tucked their kids into bed and kissed them goodnight before heading out for a quick meal. Winter break was approaching and they may even have been making plans for it as a family before leaving for dinner. They would never have thought that they wouldn't return. By sheer unfortunate luck, they found themselves in the path of blind terror that night. And now, their innocent, beautiful young kids would have to spend the rest of their lives without them.

My husband looked at me with tears in his eyes. We both struggled to take in the news.

We debated about whether or not to break the news to our son. He was only five at that time. How much would he even understand? But we didn't want a situation where he heard about it on the playground from another child and decided it would be best if we told him ourselves.

As he sat on my lap, my husband and I told him that there had been some 'people with guns' who had done some 'very bad things' in the city and 'hurt' a lot of people. We told him that his friend's parents had unfortunately been 'very badly hurt' and that his friend would not be seeing them again.

He listened silently as we spoke to him, all the while looking down at his hands. He nodded when I asked him if he understood what we were saying. We asked him how he was feeling and if he had anything that he wanted to ask us.

He said nothing for a while and continued to stare down at his hands. After a while, he climbed off my lap and went to his room to colour a drawing. My initial thought was that his innocent five-year-old mind had not been able to comprehend the enormity of the situation.

'He's far too young to understand this,' I said.

'And his friend is far too young to have to live his life without his parents,' said my husband softly.

A few hours later, our son came up to us and said he had some questions. We told him to ask us anything he wanted.

His questions hit us like a ton of bricks.

His first question was, 'But he is such a good boy and he plays soccer so well, so how could something so bad happen to him?' He was referring to his friend.

After all, don't we always try to teach our kids that good things happen to good people? So how could we explain that something so terrible had happened to an innocent child? We told him that sometimes things were just not fair, and terrible things happened to very nice people.

His next question was, 'So, can he never speak with his parents again? They do so much for him and love him so much. Will he never be able to see them again?'

Yes, we said. They won't be there in person and he won't be able to see them, but they will forever live on in his heart and the hearts of his brother and sister. He nodded and his wide eyes seemed to suggest the confusion and perhaps even the fear he was feeling.

The extent of that fear became apparent in the next question—'Can this happen to both of you? Can the bad guys shoot you? Will I never be able to see you then?' I stumbled for words. How do you address the fears of an innocent child without making promises that may be false in this uncertain world in which we live? If the attack had happened on another night or in another neighbourhood, it could just as easily have been my husband and I who were shot dead by the terrorists.

We held our son close and told him that we would try our best to stay safe and would always be there for him and his brother and sister. We didn't know what would happen in the future but we would always love him.

I was sad and angry that day. My heart ached for those three young children—wonderful, loving kids who were orphaned in a split second. I was terribly angry with the people who had turned the lives of these kids upside down and robbed them of a happy childhood with this blind and cowardly act of violence. I was sad for the many grieving families that were enduring this heartbreaking situation. And I was sad that we had to cast a shadow of fear on the sweet innocence of our child.

The next day, a counsellor came to my son's school to address all the kindergarten students and their parents. Many of the children knew by then about the terrible loss their dear friend had suffered. The children sat in a circle around the counsellor while the parents stayed towards the back of the room. The counsellor asked them to share their thoughts and the clear straightforward thinking of five- and six-year-olds came forth. The children spoke about how the 'bad people' should have used their words instead of their hands. As one of them said, talking could have helped them figure things out. All of them agreed that hurting someone else was bad and never justified. And they all said that they wanted to write a note to their friend to tell him that they were sorry that he was sad.

We looked at the children and marvelled at their innocence and their maturity. If only the world were as straightforward as kindergarten. As we grow up, we make our lives and our motivations more complicated and convoluted. Instead of expressing our feelings and talking about them, we mask them behind artificial smiles. Instead of shaking hands after a tussle on the playground and putting it behind ourselves, we carry forth the seeds of resentment in our heart. Somewhere along the way, we forget the first lesson that was taught in kindergarten—'Use your words, not your hands.'

If only we could all remember that lesson as adults. The world would be a very different place.

25: Organizationally Challenged

Picking up after young kids is like raking leaves in a backyard just before an incoming storm. It is back to square one, or worse, before you know it. You can neatly organize all their bedtime books by height, put all their toy cars and dolls in the right shelves, sort all the crayons by colour into boxes; and wipe the finger paint marks off the wall. The next day, their room will once again look like a tornado-hit area.

You wage a futile battle against loose sheets of paper, dismembered parts of toys, caps that have been estranged from their matching pens, and open jars of play dough. You overinvest in organizational aids such as toy baskets and chests. That helps in transferring the mess on the floor into a black box where, at least, it is out of sight.

The toy chest is a treasure trove in our home. Every few months, we empty it out to find things that have long been forgotten—a headless doll may emerge or an action figure that was once revered. We may also find a mouldy piece of pizza or a puzzle piece that has been missing for weeks. Unfortunately, by that time, tired of looking for it, we would have discarded the rest of the puzzle.

That is another mystery of puzzle pieces. Why is it that all five jigsaw puzzles in the home will each have exactly one piece missing? Why couldn't just one of them have five pieces missing? Who is this puzzle piece thief lurking in the home who craves exactly one piece from each puzzle, usually the one that belongs right in the middle of the picture?

In the early years of parenthood, the disorganization spreads to other parts of the home as well. Time is a precious resource and that makes previously regular purging sessions few and far between. Filing important documents or putting things away diminish in priority when there is a crying infant to comfort. As a result, you are perpetually looking for something you believed you had put in a very 'safe' place. Unfortunately, you are more likely to find the missing bib in the filing cabinet rather than the document that you are searching for.

Your sleep-deprived state also doesn't make for good memory power. Even though you have made a grocery store list, somewhere between checking the refrigerator to see what was needed and writing that down on a slip of paper, you forget a few things. Once you get home from the grocery store, you try to ingeniously make mashed potatoes without any butter.

The toddler years are the trickiest. Not only do the little brats wreak havoc in their own rooms but they also leave a path of destruction in their wake through the rest of the home. Every parent I know has, on at least one occasion, stepped on a squeaky toy in the middle of the night and scared the life out of every other adult in the house.

Toddlers also have an insatiable curiosity about what lies in handbags, briefcases and dressers. They will seize any opportunity to empty the contents from those bags or shelves and strew them across the house. DVDs and CDs will part from their cases time and time again. Your favourite shade of lipstick will be found without its cover, bent out of shape and completely unusable unless you are getting ready for Halloween. There will be moments when an awful realization will dawn on you that the sheet of paper your child is colouring on is an important bank or legal document.

You will tire of this daily game of cleaning up. Your children will not tire of wreaking havoc.

You will go through what I call the four stages of 'reactions to child-inflicted destruction': shock, anger, self-harm, and pleading for respite. It starts off with shock at the latest discovery of damage and develops into yelling at the offenders. Once you realize that your screams are not having any measurable impact on them, you sit down and tear your hair out. And soon, after a few such instances, you give up, get down on your knees and plead with them to show mercy.

Some of us will attain nirvana in this area. That is the stage when you just stop worrying about the mess that is rapidly multiplying before you and achieve a calm, almost Zen-like attitude towards it all. Your kids will look at you a little strangely at first—and then go back to whatever they are destroying at that point. Before you master nirvana, you will keep snapping back to old habits and slip into one of the stages described above. However, over time and with continued practice, you will attain the peaceful stage of not caring about the broken toys, strewn pieces of paper and handprints on the wall.

Of course, just make sure to put your passports and other important documents away safely first.

26: The Great Retail Gender Divide

It isn't the extra X chromosome that predisposes women to love shopping. Rather, it is a conditioning that begins early in infancy.

If you've ever been inside a children's clothing store, you know exactly what I am talking about. Approximately 95 per cent of the store is filled with 'new creations' and 'latest designs' for girls. And on one rack, relegated to the back corner of the store, you can find some jeans and T-shirts for boys.

If you want some variety for your son, you can get jeans in blue or black, or shirts with or without collars. If you're in a well-stocked and progressive kids wear store, you might even find button-down shirts in two different colours. But don't expect anything more. Parents in the boys' section can make a quick choice from the limited selection and head over to the cash register. They are done with shopping for their son in less than five minutes.

In contrast, the girls' section is filled with colourful outfits in myriad styles and patterns. A number of little girl mannequins will help guide (and sometimes confuse) your choices. Does the floral blouse look cuter with the embroidered pants or the layered skirt? There is a huge selection of dresses in every cut, fabric and colour, with leggings to match. And to complete the picture of a perfectly dressed little girl, there is a range of accessories such as bracelets, hair ties and sandals. Incidentally, this section also has jeans and T-shirts. Only the jeans are cuter with cuffs and embroidery. Parents—mostly moms—will gush with delight over all the choices and spend an inordinate amount of time (and money) figuring out the perfect outfits and accessories for their little girls. Total time taken at the store for them can easily cross a few hours.

I was observing all of this in a kids wear store, when it dawned on me that we were conditioning the shopping behaviour of boys and girls for life. What these little kids saw on shopping trips at the age of two was going to influence their adult behaviour and even their relationships.

For instance, if you look at adult shoppers in a mall, it is easy to separate them into a few different groups. Group A consists of two or more women. They view shopping as a fun activity, an adventure of sorts. They go into each store that catches their eye, try on something that they weren't looking for in the first place and buy something that they don't need. The group shows complete interest in each other's selections and offers encouragement and advice.

Group B consists of two or more men. They are at the mall for an express purpose and their goal is to get out of there as soon as that purpose is accomplished. No distractions for them. They just need a pair of blue trousers. Perhaps socks, if there is a special discount on them, but that's it. Detractors in this group are sternly scolded and told to stay true to the goal at hand—buy the necessary item and, without any further ado, exit the mall.

Group C, which consists of a couple shopping together,

is quite interesting. If you observe the man, he is constantly checking his watch and making exasperated expressions every time his female companion takes a detour into yet another store. It's quite clear from his face that he would much rather be sitting on the couch in front of the television than carrying bags around in the mall. He stares enviously at the group of men who have entered and exited the mall in less time than his companion has spent in perusing the clothes on a single rack in a store. From his companion's perspective, she's probably more than a little annoyed that he's not more involved and engaged in selecting candle-stands for their living-room.

Are men and women conditioned for this behaviour from childhood? After all, little boys who accompany their parents to the kids wear stores observe them going in and coming out in a matter of minutes. With young boys, even the mothers don't spend any time dilly-dallying amongst the selection. After all, choosing between two colours can only take so much time.

The girls, on the other hand, have memories of twirling around in different dresses in changing rooms. They remember their mothers debating whether to get them the pink dress or the fuchsia one, and then coordinating the hair accessories. They see shopping as something fun rather than as a chore that must be completed in order to not go to school in calf-length jeans.

Perhaps, if kids wear retailers were to expand the selection of boys apparel, future generations of men and women would be better aligned in their behaviour towards shopping. It would make a couple more likely to enjoy an afternoon together at a mall and go a long way towards supporting marital bliss.

And it would make pretty good business sense for the retailers too.

27: In Search of the Elusive Balance

Several women, including myself, try hard to find that magical and often elusive balance between family and career. We chase it incessantly by redefining roles and resetting expectations—both ours and those of others. We negotiate flexibility at work and outsource household chores in an attempt to achieve it. We remain doggedly in pursuit of that nirvana where we can remain stimulated in our careers while being there for our families; and we dream of the day when a clean, organized home and decently groomed and well-raised children can coexist in harmony with a carefully crafted business strategy and increasing sales numbers.

But is there really a happy balance? Or is it more of a compromise that leaves many women hanging in the middle, struggling to get a toehold in their dual roles?

A decision many working mothers have to make, at some point, is whether to continue to work or stay home with the kids. This decision point may come when the children are physically needy infants, tantrum-throwing toddlers, inquisitive kids, emotional tweens or hormonal teenagers. But for nearly every working mother (and many fathers as well), there comes a time in their careers when they wonder if they should continue to step on the gas pedal or if they should slow down the pace to spend more time with their children.

For some mothers, there isn't a choice. For financial, family or societal reasons, the decision to either work or be home with the kids is made for them. However, millions of mothers around the world are fortunate to have a choice. A choice that is possible due to the relentless efforts of pioneering women in prior generations, who broke through many barriers to win the right to pursue their dreams outside of the home.

Ironically, this choice is often what tears the current generation of mothers apart. Because having a choice also means making conscious compromises.

If you choose to be a working mother, you face the battle of the balance on a daily basis. Sometimes, that means having to say 'no' to assignments and roles that you desperately want to pursue. You know that the new project will challenge you and help you gain skills that will be important for your career growth. But you weigh that against the cost of more hours away from home. Perhaps, you feel guilty for even entertaining the thought of putting your career ahead of the family. And so, you tell your boss that the project you would otherwise have given your right arm for and the one that you are ideally suited for, should be given to someone else in the organization.

The trade-offs continue in your personal life. You miss school events in order to make a meeting at work or to complete a pending project. You come home to a child who tearfully tells you that you were the *only* mother who wasn't there to see the elementary school play. Racked with guilt, you profusely apologize to your child who runs away to her room to sob into her pillow. Your husband puts a reassuring hand on your shoulder and tells you that it will be fine. You bite your tongue to avoid snapping at him and silently resent him for not having to deal with the same set of expectations. Your child is ecstatic if Daddy makes it to the play, but seems to understand if he can't. Where's the fairness in that?

You sigh and swear at the school organizers who scheduled the play at two in the afternoon. Sometimes, it feels like everyone is conspiring against you.

You go to bed at night exhausted and emotionally weary. You've been up since the crack of dawn and have optimized every minute of the day. You've eaten all your meals at your desk and politely declined all after-work social events because they don't fit in your list of priorities. You've rushed home to make it in time for dinner and to help with bath, homework and bed. And you're one of the *luckier* ones, with help for other domestic chores.

Sometimes, you compare yourself to a hamster on a wheel. Running desperately, although you're not sure what the prize at the end is, or when, if ever, you'll be able to get off the darn wheel. But you're too scared to stop running, because if you do, the precariously balanced system that you have going will fall to pieces.

So you wake up early the next morning, ready to start all over again. Ready to face another day and the battle of compromises that it will bring.

Several of my role models have been working mothers. These extremely successful women around the world have risen to leadership levels in their organizations despite challenges and have proved their intellect and capabilities over and over again in male dominated industries, while raising children. They have been pioneers in their fields and have shown the path and even held the door open for other women.

But undoubtedly, these women would have faced trade-offs in their lives too. They would also have missed out on key events and milestones in their children's lives. They might also have passed on attractive work assignments for the sake of their families. We don't always hear about the professional and personal sacrifices made by women at the top, but that doesn't mean they didn't make them.

Several years ago, I attended a women's leadership conference in New York. One of the keynote speakers was a remarkably successful CFO of a large multinational company. She spoke eloquently about her rise through the ranks and her perseverance and commitment. Sitting in the audience, I was inspired and motivated by her journey. Her message to the women present was to dream big and to believe in themselves. Towards the end of her talk, the moderator asked her if she had any regrets or if she would change anything about her journey. With barely a moment's pause, the CFO replied, 'I wish I was there more for my daughters when they were growing up.' You could hear a pin drop in the auditorium as those present registered the personal sacrifice that had been made by the speaker.

It isn't easier for women who choose to quit the workforce and become stay-at-home mothers. I have met several highly qualified women who left exciting and challenging jobs as lawyers, bankers, consultants, doctors and corporate executives to be home with their children. While that was a choice they made, I suspect that when they were in college working hard towards their degrees and career aspirations, none of them imagined that they would have to make that decision. And while none of them second-guessed their choice to stay home with their kids, there was often an undercurrent of bitterness when we discussed the direction that our professional lives had taken. Bitterness at having believed for years that we could have it all and then waking up to the harsh realization that it wasn't true.

And perhaps, that is one of the biggest surprises that so many women face after having kids. We've been raised in a world where we are told that we can have it all. I come from a family of three girls and my parents always told us that we were no different than boys. We were told that as long as we were committed to our work and persevered with our efforts, we could achieve whatever it was that we desired. We were the 'new age women' who could 'have it all', we were told.

Only, we couldn't.

Once you have a family of your own, you realize that something has to give. It just isn't possible to have it all.

I have been a working mom and a stay-at-home mom. Both choices were right for me at different stages of my life and my children's ages. But neither choice, whether it was being at home with my child or trying to advance in my career, was an easy decision. I was caught in the crosshairs, making compromises in one and feeling guilty about the other.

Before becoming a mother, I had always assumed that I would continue to work after having children. Thousands of women before me had done that and shown the path. With only a few years of experience, I also worried about putting my career on hold at an early stage. If I took a break too soon, getting back into the workforce after a few years would be an uphill task.

This is another truth of motherhood. The career trajectory and women's body clocks are not aligned with each other. Our body clocks tick louder and louder as we approach key inflection points in our career trajectory, as if daring us to ignore them. A reminder of why we can't have it all.

My first career break came a little unexpectedly, following our move to India. Immediately after relocating to Mumbai, I looked for a role that would suit my career interests and also afford me the flexibility to settle my young children into their new environment.

A few months of searching resulted in many interesting positions, but none with any flexibility. While a few prospective employers understood my need for balance, most were wary about setting the wrong precedent for other women in the company.

'We'd like you to join us, but on a full-time basis. If we make flexible arrangements for you, we'll have to offer it to the other women as well,' was a response I heard more than once.

I was rather taken aback by that. That logic did not resonate with me. I thought that companies would want to provide their women (and male) employees with options that would enable them to be more engaged in their jobs in the long term, rather than worry about setting precedents. Unfortunately, this was not a sentiment that was commonly shared in Mumbai office corridors during the time of my job search.

Unwilling and unable at that time to compromise on flexibility, I took a career break. With three young children at home, the break was anything but a 'break'. The role of a stay-at-home mom was an intense 24/7 one with no days off. On any given day, there were noses to wipe, scrapes to kiss, teeth to brush, stories to read, hugs to share, meals to plan and tantrums to manage. It was physically demanding but emotionally fulfilling.

I enjoyed the luxury of time with my children during

my career break. I didn't have to constantly check my mobile device for messages. There was no external pressure or deadline that took me away from spending quality and quantity time with my children and actively participating in their growing up stages. I didn't have to worry about missing milestones with my youngest child. I was there when she said her first words and took her first set of faltering steps. I was there to accompany my middle son to play dates and music classes. I could attend every single school event in which my older child participated. He never had to look at the sea of faces in the audience and wonder whether his mother would show up or not. I saw my children thriving on the attention and time that I could provide them.

Life was good.

Except for that nagging anxiety.

When I took a break, I knew it was temporary. I was hitting the pause button and intended to return to work. As I neared the two-year mark, I started to get anxious. What if the gap on my résumé became too long to explain in a job interview? What if my skills eroded? With businesses evolving faster than ever, would my experience be relevant by the time I was ready to get back into the workforce? Would those problem-solving skills that were gained through years of hard work now be used for matching missing socks as they came out of the laundry or completing jigsaw puzzles for toddlers?

We live in a world where we are defined by our business cards. At any social event, one of the first questions you are asked by someone you've just met is on what you do for a living. I had more than a few such instances when someone would ask me what I did, and upon discovering that I was 'just a mom', their eyes would glaze over me to scan the room for other more interesting (i.e., professionally employed) people. Surely, they couldn't waste their valuable networking time on a stay-at-home mom. More than the awkwardness at these events, which I learned to ignore, it was the feeling of unfulfilled potential that started to gnaw at me.

Over the course of my career break, I read about the accomplishments of my former colleagues and classmates. I was happy for them, but also strangely envious. I couldn't help but compare my professional path and subsequent detour with theirs. One day, I came across the social media profile of a female classmate who seemed to be making both work and family possible while planning the most incredible vacations, which she documented on her home page. I wondered that if she could do it, why wasn't I even trying?

After a two-year hiatus, I decided that I wanted to jump back into the workforce, a decision that my husband supported. Having the backing of family is crucial and something that I have had the liberty of taking for granted.

After my last job search experience in India, I was a little wary about what to expect this time around. I did more homework and focused my search on companies where key management embodied values that I admired and respected. As I expected, the 'issue' of the two-year break in my career came up in every single conversation. For some interviewers, it was a matter of identifying how I had managed to remain updated with the industry during that time. But for others, it was a question of the choice that I had made.

And the latter always bothered me. Why did I need to explain my decision to prioritize my children over a job? Why did I need to have a 'story' about what else I was doing during that time? I understood the concern that an organization might have regarding the current relevance of my skills and knowledge base, but I did not understand their puzzlement over my decision to spend more time with my children at the expense of my career.

After a few months, I accepted an exciting role with a company that I admired and respected. Not only was the job stimulating, it was also largely predictable in terms of the working hours.

I returned to work recharged. With the help of a supportive spouse and a good nanny, I was back at work and loving the new challenge.

I thoroughly enjoyed the intellectual stimulation, the ability to interact with diverse, interesting and smart people and even the opportunity of enjoying a cup of hot coffee at my desk. (During my time as a stay-at-home mom, I couldn't remember a single instance of being able to finish a cup of coffee without being interrupted by at least one of the children.) With fairly manageable work hours, I was also able to combine a productive day at work with quality time at home with my children in the evening.

I was thrilled at being able to achieve the balance. Of course, there were compromises made again in the quest for balance—missed sports events, drama performances and more—but that was a choice that I had made. I had accepted that I couldn't have it all.

A few years later, the situation changed. One of my children went through a tough phase at school and needed more of my presence. He wanted to talk about certain issues with me when he came home from school, but I wasn't there. By the time I reached home in the evenings, he had stewed in his thoughts for hours and was often too upset to even talk about the issue anymore. The stress that he was undergoing was slowly but surely impacting him.

I watched the situation with my son and hoped that it would sort itself out. His teachers were supportive, but no one could replace me in his life at that stage. There were days when he seemed to retreat into a shell, and I was sick with worry about him.

I found myself being concerned about him when I was at work, and being stressed about work when I was with the children. And I recognized that the situation was not sustainable. Did I want to 'lean in' at work? Of course I did. I am ambitious about my career and want to succeed in it. But I wasn't ready to compromise on my child's happiness and confidence to make it happen. I couldn't make that choice.

I saw the look on people's faces when I told them that I was leaving to spend more time with my children.

It was a confused and puzzled expression.

'Your children are older now. You managed to make it work for the last several years. Why can't that just continue?' I heard this question many times.

Women had the most interesting reaction. Some of the working mothers even felt like I was betraying them. We were each other's support group. One of them asked if I could have tried harder to make it all work.

Perhaps I could have, I told her. But I didn't *want* to try harder. I didn't want to always be the hamster on the wheel.

Other women understood. Some of them had been in similar situations themselves and had either taken breaks or ploughed ahead. Regardless, they all knew the heartbreak that I was experiencing.

I was keenly aware that stepping off the career highway a

second time could be suicidal for my future aspirations. I had managed, after the first break, to find a job that I loved. But it hadn't been easy. Giving it all up again did seem foolhardy.

I left knowing that I might get another chance to get back on the career track, or I might not. But I knew, for sure, that I would not get another chance to be actively involved in my children's early lives. If I didn't achieve my career aspirations, I could deal with it. But if I screwed up my role as a mother, I'd be rather disappointed with myself.

And so, the quest for that elusive balance continues.

28: Thinking Ahead to Those Teenage Years

Even before my daughter was born, I had decided not to pierce her ears as a newborn.

In India, where it is traditional to pierce a baby girl's ears within the first few weeks of her birth, I was constantly asked why I had not done the same. Friends and family told me that it was better to pierce the ears early on when it didn't hurt babies as much. I'm not sure that's been factually proven—I think it's just that babies can't tell you how much it hurts them.

To all of them, my answer for putting off the traditional ear piercing was that her two-year-old brother was likely to pull at a shiny metal stud in her ear and cause her pain repeatedly. The answer seemed to satisfy most people as logical enough.

But the honest reason for the delay is that I *want* her to feel and remember the pain of getting her ears pierced.

While the pain of a piercing will last for just a few minutes, I hope the realization of it will give her reason to pause when she is tempted to get piercings on *other* parts of her body.

I hope that when she pauses, she'll remember the tender oil massages that her mother gave her. I hope she remembers those before she enters a tattoo parlour and forever changes the way her body looks.

I hope that when she stops to think, she'll remember the kisses her mother gave her on the forearm. That same forearm on which she is considering getting a permanent tattoo that states '*REBEL*'.

I hope that when she thinks about it for a moment, she will remember the sun block and moisturizer that her mother gently applied on her face every day in order to protect her skin from any damage. I hope she remembers that before she decides to pierce her tongue, upper lip or eyebrow.

I know the pain of the ear piercing will be momentary, but I am hoping that pausing to think about it will help her remember. I hope she will respect her body and not follow a temporary fad just for the sake of fitting in.

So, I am going to wait to pierce my daughter's ears until she is older, so that as a teenager when she considers getting a tattoo or piercing her tongue, eyebrow, navel or other body part, she thinks long and hard about it.

And if after thinking it through, she still decides to get a tattoo or piercings to express herself in a way that I am not able to understand, I am fine with it. At least, she thought about it.

29: Travelling with Kids

It all begins with the planning.
There might have been a time when you vacationed in barely heard of, tucked away locations that were far off the beaten path, and immersed yourself in a new culture in a completely different part of the world. The further away the destination was from the humdrum and activity of the city, the more attractive it was to you. The goal was to discover and experience something that even *Lonely Planet* hadn't.

Now, when it's time to plan family vacations, you pick 'child-friendly' destinations, which are less than a four-hour direct flight away. 'Child-friendly' is essentially code for places that are teeming with tourists and nauseatingly filled with commercially driven activities targeted towards the under-eight age group.

In your previous travels, you stayed at quaint little inns, tucked away from the beaten path, where fresh local fare would be served along with interesting conversation every morning. Local history and culture would seep in through every painting on the wall and each artefact on the counter would have a story of its own. The thrill of learning something new about the place excited you and the element of surprise in your travels was seductive.

But that was before the kids came along.

Now, you peruse the website of one of the global hotel chains where everything will be *exactly* as mandated in the hotel's manual. You are virtually guaranteed that the room, down to the bedspread, curtains and towels, will be identical to the one that you see on the website. The decorations in the room are unique to *nowhere*, but a mini refrigerator and microwave are available. The hotel has a child-friendly swimming pool (with a maximum depth of no more than two feet), and the giant bowl of flavoured lollipops in the lobby is refreshed daily. The breakfast menu includes pancakes, and Goofy and Pooh make visits on weekends.

You click on the 'Book Now' icon.

How the mighty have fallen.

Then comes the packing. If you were going away by yourself for a few days, you may have packed a couple of pairs of jeans, a few shirts and some basic toiletries. Most of the time, everything you needed would fit in a carry-on bag and you wouldn't have to deal with checking in any luggage—something many of us try to avoid even more than the plague.

Now, try packing for kids. Interestingly, there is an inverse relationship between the age of the child and the weight of the luggage that you need to carry for them. Simply put, the younger the kid, the more the paraphernalia. You need to make allowances for the many spit-ups, diaper leaks, food spills and mud stains, and budget a minimum of three to four outfits for each child per day. Now, add to it the diapers, extra food (in case the hotel uses a different brand of pancake mix or pasta) and numerous toiletries (non-fluoride toothpaste for baby, gentle shampoo for baby, gentle soap for baby, face cream for baby, body cream for baby, hand cream for baby, butt cream for baby, etc.).

Very soon, instead of a small overnighter, you've got a supersized suitcase.

Repeat the packing steps above for each additional child.

Of course, the supersized suitcases now have no space left for your jeans and T-shirts.

After multiple checks and rechecks of luggage, passports, tickets, you're ready to leave for the airport.

You get to the check-in counter and the nice lady asks if you'd all like to sit together. No, you reply, we really wouldn't like to sit with these kids, but we don't think we have a choice.

The nice lady asks you if anyone else has given you anything to pack.

Nope, you shrug, as you look at the bulging bags. Hard to believe but they're all ours.

Have your bags been out of your sight at any time?

You raise your eyebrows at the nice lady. You think to yourself, 'Have you tried to get three kids fed, bathed, clothed and out of the house? Do you think you can do that while dragging bags along?' But you bite your tongue, smile and say, 'No, not even for a moment.'

You get your boarding passes and see that once again, you've been relegated to the back of the aircraft. And the kids are seated next to you.

Great.

Now, off to security where you need to somehow ensure that the kids stay with you in line. So you hold their wrists with a vice-like grip as they squirm around, trying to wriggle free. After over twenty minutes of trying to keep the kids in order by requesting, coercing, threatening and pleading with them, you finally get to the front of the line. At that very moment, the toddler who has very recently been toilet trained tugs on your shirtsleeve and announces that he needs to go to the bathroom.

You stare incredulously at your spouse. This cannot be happening. He shakes his head and says, 'Murphy's Law.'

Who is this Murphy and why does he hate you so much?

A quick scan reveals that getting out of the security line to take him to the bathroom will virtually guarantee that you will miss your flight.

You promise the little boy two candy bars if he can just hold on for two minutes longer. You're at the front of the line now and start getting the sneakers and jackets off the kids. The youngest one starts giggling as she thinks it's time for her bath and starts asking for her rubber duck. 'Baa, Baa,' she says.

'It's quack, quack,' says her over-smart older brother.

Meanwhile, your toddler son is hopping around trying to keep from peeing in the middle of security check. You fervently hope he doesn't pee right there as it has just occurred to you that that may be the fastest way to get on the 'No Fly' list.

You manage to clear security, leave your husband to gather the belongings from the scanner, while you scoop up the toddler and run to the nearest washroom. As you stare at the long line snaking outside the women's room, you know you have to up the ante.

'Four candy bars,' you say to your son, as you huff and puff your way towards the washroom. 'Please, hold on just a little longer.'

But you know there's no way he's going to make it. So you stop, reach into the diaper bag, pull a diaper out, peel down your son's pants in the middle of the airport terminal, and wrap the diaper around him.

'Go. Just go in the diaper.'

You see the surprise in his eyes. YOU want him to use the diaper! What about all the weeks of toilet training that you and he have just gone through? You have a flashback to those tears of joy and whoops of jubilation when he went in the toilet for the first time all by himself.

You really want him to use that diaper?

You look wearily at the long line outside the restroom and you know it's a losing battle.

'Just use it, kid.'

After a pause, he says, 'Will I still get the candy bars?' And unable to hold on any longer, he uses the diaper.

Reunited with the rest of the family, you trek towards the assigned gate. As you enter the plane, you see the panicked expressions on the faces of passengers with empty seats next to them. You can even hear a couple of people whispering anxious prayers, 'Please, not them. Please, not them. I'll take the 200-kilogram person behind them, but please, not the kids!' As you pass their row, an audible sigh of relief is heard. They even greet the 200-kilogram person who squeezes into his seat and half of theirs as if he were a long-lost friend.

You make your way back to row 42, pushing one kid in front of you while holding another on your hip and trying to squeeze the oversized diaper bag through the aisle. Finally, you reach your seats. The kids argue for a few minutes over who is going to take the window seat.

'It's my turn!'

'He had it last time too.'

'Did not.'

'Did too!'

Husband steps in and physically lifts and lowers one duelling child into the window seat and the other into the aisle seat.

Fabulous—that means you get the middle seat. The other two members of the family take the seats across the aisle.

You lean back, completely worn out. The vacation hasn't started and you're ready to go back to your own bed. The tugging on your sleeves from both sides begins. Both of them declare that they are bored. The doors of the airplane haven't even closed yet and they're already restless. This could be a very long flight. But then, thankfully, the electronic gods come to the rescue. Each of the kids is handed a fully charged electronic device loaded with age appropriate games. And like magic, silence follows.

You look over at your spouse and smile. You still have several hours before you reach your destination, but you've made it past the first hurdle. You open up the *Lonely Planet* guide to read about the cultural highlights of your destination. You read it in the vain hope that there may be some room in your itinerary amidst all the 'child-friendly activities' to see the things that you want to see.

You turn to see the kids engrossed in their devices and thank the electronic gods again. If you're truly fortunate and the timing of the meal service on the plane is good, the kids may even take a nap on the flight.

Fortunately, our oldest son doesn't have much of a problem falling asleep on flights. The only problem is that he is a heat-seeking missile who gravitates towards the person next to him, often seeking the softest part of the person's upper torso for comfort. There have been times when we've been seated next to his younger siblings and he's had to sit with a complete stranger across the aisle. Barely an hour into the flight, he's nestled against his neighbour's body. I will always be grateful to the many gracious fellow passengers who have taken care of my son for the duration of the flight, while he buried his head in their armpits.

Speaking of kids and fellow passengers, we've all been in planes with screaming toddlers. Most of them are accompanied by exasperated and frustrated parents who have done just about everything to calm down their young ones, while receiving dirty looks from many others on the plane. They've walked their young child up and down endlessly in the aisles, contorted themselves into all sorts of shapes to retrieve the little teddy that Junior kept throwing under the seat, and played 'peek-a-boo' games constantly to keep their child happy and the volume levels reasonable in the cabin. Regardless of how successful they were on keeping their little one happy and reasonably calm on the flight, I have nothing but respect and a tremendous amount of empathy for these parents.

But then, I have also been on planes with parents who couldn't care less as their young one kicked the seat-back of the person sitting in front of them, threw his food across the cabin, or ran rampant through the aisle while elbowing other passengers in their seats. I have watched as the parents just sat in their seats with their earphones on. It has made me want to get up and smack the parents. The only thing I would say to them is, 'Turn that movie off, get off your backside and take care of that child right now!' When you sign up to become a parent, you submit to losing all remnants of high altitude peace. You cannot hide behind earphones and a movie screen while your child wreaks havoc on an airplane.

The pilot makes the landing announcement. The children

are looking out of the windows in amazement at the new city that they will be visiting for the next few days. They excitedly point at the buildings that they can see from their plane seats. Their enthusiasm is infectious and you start to look forward to seeing the city through the eyes of your children.

What could any travel book ever tell you about that?

But for now, you brace yourself for the madness of the baggage claim area.

30: Guilt–the Constant Companion

Guilt has a middle name. It's called Motherhood.

Guilt has been a constant companion in my parenting journey. It never lets down, never eases up and never takes a day off. It stays with me all the time. It holds my hand and caresses it gently to remind me of its gnawing presence every single day.

It moved in soon after I first found out that I was pregnant. After the initial excitement, I was stricken with guilt over the two glasses of wine and a plate of sushi that I had consumed the week before the positive pregnancy test. What if something happened to the baby's brain development because of the wine? What if the raw fish in the sushi had somehow affected the baby? How would I ever be able to live with myself?

That was the guilt that I felt nine months *before* I became a mother. Ever since then, guilt and I have been joined at the hip. It rises with me every single morning and plays with my subconscious mind long after I have fallen asleep.

I am not the only one stalked by guilt. This unwelcome guest who shows no sign of leaving affects most mothers. Its clones live in homes around the world. Whenever a baby is born, guilt follows closely but surely behind.

I don't believe there is one particular thing about being a mother that encourages or stimulates guilt. It is *every* single thing.

I felt guilty when I bottle-fed my children. I felt guilty when I let my infant son cry it out. I felt guilty when I let my children co-sleep. I felt guilty when I left them alone in their cribs.

I felt guilty when I let them stay up past their bedtime. I felt guilty when I didn't wake up bright and early with them on weekends.

I felt guilty about using the television or electronic device as a proxy babysitter.

I felt guilty when I went to work. I felt guilty when I stayed home.

I felt guilty about ignoring my errands or my work when I played with my children. I felt guilty about neglecting them when I did anything else.

I felt guilty if I went on a date night with my husband and left the children behind. If I didn't, I felt guilty about not spending time with him.

If I slept in, I felt guilty. If I stayed out late, I felt guilty.

If my children got hurt, I felt guilty about not being more vigilant. If they fell sick, I felt guilty about not taking care of them well enough.

I felt guilty whenever I did anything for myself.

If I spent time alone with one child, I felt guilty about not being with the other two. If I spent time with all of them together, I felt guilty about not giving them individualized attention.

If I helped them with their homework, I worried that I was spoon-feeding them. If I didn't help them, I felt that I was not staying involved.

The bottom line is that as a mother, you are the living embodiment of guilt. Twenty-four hours a day, seven days a week—you are feeling guilty about something. And if you're not, you feel guilty about not feeling guilty. It's a no-win situation.

I asked my mother how she had dealt with the omnipresent maternal guilt. She gave me a blank look.

'What guilt?' she asked. 'Our generation didn't overthink and overanalyze everything as your generation does. We did what we could. We made do with what we had. And that was it. There was no question of any guilt.'

I marvelled and envied the simplicity and confidence with which she described her journey of raising three children, while working and managing with far fewer resources than I had at my disposal.

But she was right. We overanalyze our roles as mothers. We examine every action that we take or don't take under a microscope. We set the bar high for ourselves, and on the occasions when we meet it, we reset the bar even higher. That's what our constant companion, guilt, makes us do. It keeps whispering the phrase 'not good enough' in our ears.

We are also a generation of mothers that seeks external validation of our efforts. The wide-eyed excitement and joy shown by our children at the lopsided homemade birthday cake are not enough for us. So we put ourselves up for judgment in the court of social media. We post pictures, tell our stories, share our fears and insecurities, and then wait patiently, or rather refresh the screen repeatedly, for comments from our friends and fellow moms. We crave their approval and their declaration of us being good mothers.

But social media can be a cruel place. It lures you in with

reassurances from others, and then just when your defences are down, it hits you with even more insecurities.

A few inches below the picture of your homemade chocolate cake, which seems to have drawn inspiration from the Leaning Tower of Pisa, sits another picture of a birthday cake. This one also claims to be homemade. It has tiny, perfectly detailed flowers in frosting around its border. The top of the cake resembles the Garden of Eden with carefully crafted sugar figurines adorning it. The mother who has made it wonders if it is good enough for her child's birthday celebration. The picture has over five hundred 'likes', the social media equivalent of a pat on the back. Yours has four.

'Not good enough. Just not good enough,' whispers that all too familiar voice in your ears.

As you scroll down the screen, the insecurities seem to double, triple and quadruple. There is someone who is chaperoning more school field trips, someone who is baking more treats, someone who is driving to more soccer camps, someone who has a more organized home, and someone who has much better hair.

'Told you. You're just not good enough,' comes the ominous whisper again.

There is always someone's child who seems to be smarter and more athletic than yours. There is always someone who is raising the next Olympian or the next Mensa candidate, while you struggle with teaching basic literacy and hand-eye coordination. So what if your children are only five years old? You're quite obviously not doing your job as their mother.

In the overly connected world that we live in, there are plenty of examples of women who are doing what you are trying to do, but better. And that doesn't help in quieting that little voice.

And so you begin to doubt yourself even more. You quake with fear at not being a worthy enough mother to your children. All your insecurities and doubts come rushing to the fore.

We stress and overanalyze every action in our quest to be the perfect mother to our children. When all they need is their own relaxed and happy mother with all her flaws and imperfections.

But where's the fun in that? Getting toothless smiles and hugs from our children as they appreciate our lopsided culinary attempts is not enough. We, as the new age mothers, feel a desperate need to put ourselves through the wringer, time and time again.

If we truly wanted, we could evict guilt from our homes. But we also know that its presence is the reason that we try harder every single day. So that one day, hopefully, there will be a little voice that will say, 'You are good enough.'

31: Surviving the Birthday Parties

When your children are under the age of five, one of the most dreaded emails to receive in your inbox is, 'Our dear son/daughter is turning another year older and would like to invite your child to his/her birthday celebration. A paper invite will follow, but please save the date and get ready for a super fun time!'

The invite could just as easily be saying, 'In order to keep up with the Joneses, Patels, Kapoors and Smiths of the grade, we are compelled to throw a lavish, no expense spared birthday party for our little girl/boy. Please bring your child to the overly decorated venue where loud music will be blaring, myriad entertainers will be performing and waiters will be serving a never-ending supply of sugar-laden feasts and drinks to the young ones. At the end of the birthday carnival, we will be handing out expensive return presents to ensure that the kids squeal with delight and create pressure on their own parents for their upcoming birthdays. You will soon receive an over-the-top invite with embossed gold lettering. We hope your child can come to the party!'

Whatever happened to the good old birthday parties where homemade cakes, orange squash and a game of hide-and-seek were all it took for kids to have a fun time and declare the party to be a grand success?

You groan loudly as you read the invite and curse the parent who sent it to you, under your breath. The last several weekends have been punctuated with similar Disney-themed birthday parties. You wonder for a few minutes if you can just delete the email and pretend that you never received it. But you know that your son or daughter will hear about it from their friends on the playground and will be crestfallen about being the only one not to get an invite.

So you sweetly ask your child that evening, 'XYZ has a birthday party coming up. They've invited you to it, but Daddy and I were hoping we could just go somewhere as a family this weekend. Perhaps we could go for a picnic in the park or even to the movies.'

'I wanna go to the paaaaarty!!!!'

Your child's shrill response makes it abundantly clear that there is no room for negotiation on this one.

'YOU'RE taking him to this one,' you tell your child's father. 'I took him to the last one and had a migraine for hours after.'

When the kids are younger and need you to accompany them to birthday parties, these events consume most of your weekends. Little children are not particularly discerning when it comes to pruning down an attendee list and tend to invite everyone in the class. This essentially implies that nearly every other weekend is dotted with these 'super fun' events.

For parents of young kids, the birthday parties are about as 'super fun' as a proctology exam. But there is light at the end of this tunnel. Once your kids are a little older, you start looking forward to these birthday parties, where you can drop off your child and then pick him/her up after a couple of hours.

Getting two glorious hours on the weekend when you can do what you want (get a manicure or just enjoy a few hours of peace with a good book) is truly 'super fun'.

But until that glorious time, you play your role of patrol police at the birthday parties while counting down the days, or rather years, till the drop-off phase begins.

You arrive with your child at the elaborately decorated venue with the birthday child's present. There was a time when a good book or a fun board game made a great birthday present. Not anymore. Now, it's all about gifting a fancy toy or limited edition doll. And size does matter. Ever seen how broadly the child that walks into a birthday party with a gift larger than himself is smiling? He knows he's nailed it, thanks to Daddy's trip to Dubai the previous week.

I have a dirty little secret about birthday presents. There is a closet in my home that is filled with a variety of gifts that my children have received over the last few years. While it may sound cruel or even miserly to some, I see no reason why my children need a half dozen radio control cars, a dozen dolls or several different sets of the same board game. So at the end of each birthday party, they are allowed to pick a maximum of four presents that they wish to keep, while all the others go into the closet. Before you scoff, you should also know that it's not easy recycling birthday gifts. It takes a lot of attention to detail to ensure that you do not accidentally give a present back to the original giver.

But back to the birthday party. The activities start off with the kids jumping in a bouncy castle or a jungle gym, and you crane your neck to make sure that your child remains upright at all times, and if necessary, to stop other kids from jumping on his/her head. You also try to discourage the kids from eating and drinking while bouncing, because you are certain that it will not end well. Despite your intense craving for a nap (or at the least, a double espresso), you can't help smiling at the pure joy that your child is obviously experiencing by jumping around with his or her buddies.

After they have sweated enough in the jungle gym, the kids make their way to circle time activities, which are led by a party host and accompanied with loud music played by a disc jockey. Invariably, parents will be asked to join the kids in the 'hokey pokey' or 'birdy dance'. I don't know about most parents but doing the birdy dance on a Saturday afternoon is not my idea of 'super fun'.

Next up is more entertainment for the kids, often in the form of a magician or a puppeteer. Now, there are usually one or two birthday party puppeteers in any given town, and they each have about four or five different stories that they enact. So, there is a rather high probability that you and your child will have seen the puppet story being shown at least a couple of times in the past few months. However, while you think that the proctology exam would be less painful than *Jack and the Beanstalk* for the seventh time, your child is completely engrossed in the puppet show, his mouth open wide in amazement at the discovery that the little seeds grow into a large tree. It will be at times like these when you will worry about your sweet child's cognitive capabilities.

The puppet show is followed by the arrival of the birthday cake amidst huge fanfare. The children all crowd around it to marvel at the decorations and the elaborate sugar-crafted characters, while a few spunky little ones will try to lick the buttercream off the sides of the cake.

I do wish that parents of young kids would blow the candles

out for their little ones. Because Junior often doesn't have the strength (post the bouncy castle and birdy dance) to blow out five or six candles by himself and ends up spitting all over the top of the cake. Not that his friends care about that. They're still busy trying to lick the icing off the sides.

Once the cake which was embellished with finger smudges, licks and saliva has been eaten, you start the process of cajoling your child to leave the party. You're not alone in this—other weary parents are doing the same and there is a cacophony of tantrums in various corners of the party venue. The only thing that finally convinces them to leave is the promise of the return gift.

Now, I find the concept that kids need to be given gifts for *showing up* to a birthday party a little ludicrous. But the bigger issue is that many parents have taken the goody bag of candy and stickers to a whole different level. If you've ever worried that your child has brought home a return present that is considerably more expensive than the present you sent for the birthday child, you know what I mean.

There also has to be a rule against giving any living things as return presents. My oldest once came home from a birthday party in Mumbai with a goldfish. In what could only be described as a serendipitous moment of brilliance, we decided to name the goldfish 'Goldie'. With much fanfare, Goldie was given her place of honour on the side table in the living-room, where she could keep an eye on everyone while swimming in her glass bowl.

Two days later, as the kids were eating their breakfast, my son said, 'Mom, what's the matter with Goldie?' I looked over and saw her floating belly up in the water. She had died, leaving me with the task of getting grieving and howling kids to school on time.

At another birthday party, the return presents were puppies. Several parents were shocked and livid when their children came home with their new four-legged best friends. Fortunately, my kids were not invited to that party. Many of these families had to take the puppies to animal shelters, which was horrible for the innocent animals as well as the parents, who had to deal with their children's tears.

And then, there was the party where the return presents were iPads. Unfortunately (this time), my kids were not invited to that party. Several parents felt that the pressure this put on them for their own child's upcoming birthday party was completely unnecessary. They expected to go into debt when their kids went to college or got married, not when they turned seven.

Interestingly, birthday parties seem to be recession proof. The harder hit the economy, the more Mommy and Daddy want to prove to Junior that all is indeed well. Such is our need to protect our children and keep them safely ensconced in the bubbles that we wrap around them.

With the return present clutched tightly in your child's hands, you finally manage to get home for a much needed nap for both of you. However, instead of being tired after all the activity of the last couple of hours, your child, powered up with pizza, fries and sugary treats, is filled with energy that demands to be displayed.

And that's when the migraine starts.

I have had my share of 'fun' at more birthday parties than I care to recount, both in India as well as in the US. While the structure of the parties remains the same in the two countries, there were a few differences that I observed in the ones I attended.

Birthday parties in metropolitan Indian cities tend to have more extravagant decorations, more extensive game stalls, more elaborate food selection and more expensive return presents. In many ways, the preparations for the big fat Indian wedding begin with the big fat birthday parties.

Additionally, due to the affordability of live-in nannies in India, parents are able to outsource most of their birthday party responsibilities. It is common at a birthday party in Mumbai or Delhi to see a mother decked out in a Versace dress, Jimmy Choo heels and a Louis Vuitton bag coming in with her child and nanny following closely behind. One look at the mother and it is pretty clear that she will not be the one running around the jungle gym keeping a watchful eye on her son or daughter. While the moms make a social event out of the party for themselves at one table, the nannies make sure that the little ones stay safe and get enough licks of the birthday cake.

There is one thing that is universal across birthday parties in any part of the world—the harrowed expressions on the faces of the host parents. They are easily recognizable as the ones who look completely stressed and are running between activity centres, games stalls and the food tables to ensure that all children are safe and out of trouble.

As much as I cringe at the thought of attending kids' birthday parties, there are three each year that I absolutely dread.

These are the ones of my own children.

Now that our kids are in the drop-off age group, my husband and I have primary responsibility for twenty to twenty-five screaming, hyperactive children who are completely deaf to any instructions. Groups of devilishly smiling parents drop off their wards in our care and beat a hasty retreat while promising to return no earlier than the designated pick-up time, three hours later.

My husband and I usually say a prayer at the start of our children's parties. It's our way of drawing enough strength to last for the next several hours and return the various children safely to their rightful parents.

And that is not always an easy task.

My son's eighth birthday party was held at a neighbourhood restaurant which had an available activity area. I tried to be polite to the parents that were dropping off their kids and running away from the venue, while at the same time, keeping an eye on the growing number of rambunctious children in my care.

A few activities later, the children were served their drinks by the restaurant staff and were delighted at the beautiful blue-coloured beverages being offered to them.

I love a good-looking drink and said to my husband, 'I wonder how their lemon sodas are getting that pretty blue colour.' His smile suddenly froze on his face and his eyes widened in horror. 'I know only one thing that makes drinks that colour. Grab those glasses back!' he yelled.

He jumped to his feet and started snatching the drinks back from all the kids, with me close behind, nearly arm-wrestling a couple of the boys to get their glasses.

Turned out the overzealous bartender at the restaurant was putting a couple of drops of Blue Curacao into the lemon drinks to make them look more appealing to the kids. Apparently, the fellow had no idea that it had some alcohol content, which we explained to him was a rather career-limiting sort of ignorance.

Fortunately, none of the kids had had more than a sip by the time of the discovery. We would have had quite some explaining to do if we had handed over tipsy children to their parents at pick-up time.

Although, on the other hand, the silver lining would possibly have been the banning of our family from all birthday parties in the future.

I guess you win some and you lose some.

32: Don't Call Her a Supermom

I hate the term 'supermom'.
There have been a few times when I have been called that word by well-meaning acquaintances and friends.

And I have winced inwardly every single time.

'Wow! You have a career and kids and manage it all. How do you do it? You must be a supermom.'

'No, I am not a supermom!' I would say to them. 'That's a horrible thing to say. Please don't ever say that again to me or any other mother.'

I know my reaction surprised people, as they meant it as a compliment. But it was a visceral reaction. I hated being called a supermom because being a super-anything inherently means that you have it all together and are always succeeding, or at the very least, handling all your responsibilities well with grace and efficiency.

I was barely managing to keep my head above water. I was failing in my responsibilities—in one way or another—every single day.

On some days, I would miss a sports event or a drama performance that one of my children was involved in, because I had to be at work. On other days, I would rush through a work project to make it on time to the paediatrician or dentist appointment.

I was definitely falling behind in several attributes of a supermom. My kids were getting nowhere near their five daily servings of fruit and vegetables. Their birthday cakes were cobbled together from instant cake mixes and packaged frosting rather than being baked and decorated beautifully from scratch. I was hopelessly behind on hosting our fair share of play dates. I was caught hiding behind furniture in school when teachers were looking for parent volunteers for the classroom. And I wasn't checking my children's homework regularly.

There were days when I was too exhausted to help my son on a school project or to reply to a work email that needed a prompt response.

Sometimes, I would forget to read a bedtime story to my daughter. Sometimes, I would cheat and skip a page or two in the middle of the story.

It was a good day if I managed to get my children to brush their teeth and kissed them all goodnight.

I was setting the bar pretty low for myself.

Ever seen a Superhero comic where the protagonist is struggling just to keep it all together? Ever seen Superman unable to make it halfway across the city for a child's drama performance because he's stuck in traffic? (Well, perhaps he would be if his cape was stored in my disastrously disorganized closet.) Ever seen a movie in which Spiderman is curled up in bed in sheer exhaustion begging those around him to give him a few minutes of peace so he could untangle himself from his own web? Ever heard of Wonder Woman having a meltdown because she forgot to order the groceries on time and now there was no bread in the house?

On a regular basis, I was struggling to put one foot in front of the other and hoping to simply make it through the day with caffeine, prayers and the occasional Valium.

I know many other mothers, just like myself, who pour all their energy and prayers into getting through the day without any major mishaps, while looking forward to that golden moment in the evening when they can crawl into their beds, watch a few minutes of brainless television or share a few moments of peace with their partner, before recharging themselves for a new day and new battles.

Being called a supermom means that we would be judged at a much higher level. It would be like getting moved up to an advanced level in a class when you were struggling with getting the basics done right.

Would I still be able to serve macaroni and cheese dinners and use the television for babysitting in the 'supermom' category? Probably not.

Being a supermom would mean having to meet higher expectations, or at least keep the façade of meeting them. It would just add to the mountain of expectations that moms already put on themselves.

So for me, 'supermom' was not a compliment, no matter how well-meaning the intent behind it. I didn't feel like a supermom, and worse, hearing the term made me feel like I didn't even have the leeway to fail.

So do a mom a favour. Don't call her a supermom. Cut her some slack. Let her screw something up.

Remember, she's only human.

33: My Favourite Child

One of the cardinal sins a parent can commit is to have a favourite among his or her children. Even though each child is different and has their own unique personalities, the rule for parents is to love and care for each of their children in *exactly* the same measure.

I have three children and I have a favourite child.

There, I said it.

Now, shoot me for being an unfair mother. One who dares to publicly announce that she *(gasp)* has a favourite among her children. That among the equals, there is indeed one who is more favoured than the others.

For no two children can be the same. And no matter what parenting wisdom says, comparisons are bound to happen. And a *favourite* will inevitably emerge.

I have a favourite child when I need a reassuring hug. An ever-willing cuddler, this one has the softest arms, the sweetest scent and the biggest hug. With near acrobatic flexibility, this child manages to fit perfectly in my embrace, with their head nestled between my chin and shoulder. The warm breath of this favourite child on my neck is the most relaxing sensation that I have ever known.

I have a favourite child when I just want to sit with someone in silence. This child sits quietly with me as we both look out of the window at the trees, or lie next to each other while reading our books. This very mature child gives me their shoulder and wipes my silent tears on days when I am sad. And in those moments, this child never asks any questions nor makes any judgments, but simply takes my hand in theirs.

I have a favourite child who has the best sense of humour and makes me laugh on my gloomiest days. This child lights up the room by walking into it. Being serious or sad is not an option around this child whose zest and enthusiasm for life is contagious. To this child, every moment in life is a moment worth living and laughing.

My favourite child is my go-to child when I need a 'pep talk'. This one is a fighter, brimming with confidence. The courage and conviction this favourite child has shown on several occasions are an example to me. If I ever have a moment of self-doubt, this favourite child of mine will knock it out of me.

So yes, I have a favourite child.

And I daresay that every parent with more than one child has a favourite too—even if they don't confess to it.

34: Missing the 'Old' Me

There are times when I miss my old self. The person I was *before* I became a mother.

That was a time when I did things for myself, when I didn't always have the needs of others at the forefront. I could plan an evening, a weekend or a vacation based on what *I* wanted to do. And I could make those decisions at a moment's notice.

That was also a time when I could focus on what I wanted from life. I could decide on where I wanted to live and what path I wanted to pursue, while keeping only my desires and aspirations in mind.

Some of that changed when I got married, but with enough common interests as middle ground with my husband, the impact was minimal. When you choose your spouse, you have the luxury of having several conversations in advance. You have a fairly good understanding of what each of you values and is seeking from life. And even as you transition to being part of a couple, there is ample space to continue to be yourself.

But then, the kids came and everything changed. There never was an opportunity to have a similar discussion with the kids before they entered and effectively took over our lives.

Every decision now takes into account the wishes and

needs of the children on a disproportionate basis. In fact, as a rule of thumb, the weightage that any family member gets in a decision is inversely proportional to their age. So the younger they are, the greater their influence on the final family decision.

This guides 'lower impact' decisions such as movie night choices, dining selections, weekend activities and vacation picks.

If, in your pre-kids avatar, you were someone who enjoyed catching the latest action movies and socializing with friends over one or more glasses of wine at new restaurants, you may barely recognize yourself anymore. Now, on Friday evenings, you are more likely to be found decompressing from the week with a bowl of microwave popcorn, while cueing the fifteenth repeat of an animated movie and waiting for the pizza delivery to arrive.

In the initial years of parenthood, discretionary leisure activities are the first casualties.

Becoming a parent also affects the 'bigger impact' decisions such as where to live, how to educate your children, how to practise your faith, whether to pursue a career, how to stretch your finances, and much more.

Of course, this is all part of the circle of life, and when one becomes a parent, priorities and responsibilities change. And it is a change that is welcome because it brings innumerable moments of immense joy, happiness, laughter and love.

But somehow, for women in particular, this change also causes us to lose some of our individuality. Our sense of self seems to shift to our roles as mothers and primary caregivers to our children.

The decline of self is exacerbated by how the rest of

the world starts to behave with mothers. Teachers who are older than me have often addressed me as 'mom', both in the presence and absence of my children. The paediatrician, the dentist and even the neighbourhood grocer call me 'mummy'. Emails received are addressed to 'Dear so-and-so's mom', and I routinely sign off my notes as 'mom', even to those to whom I am not related.

For a while, even my husband began to address me as 'mom'. He thought that it would be less confusing for our young kids if there was consistency. I told him that if he continued with that, he should expect nothing other than motherly affection from me going forward, as that would also be less confusing for the children.

That threat helped in getting my identity back, at least with him.

Besides the identity crisis of 'me versus mom', there is also a hesitation mothers feel when pursuing any activity that is not directly connected with raising the family or managing the home.

As mothers, many of us continuously prioritize the needs of our children. In fact, as a society, we consider 'good moms' to be the ones who always put their children's needs ahead of their own, and we speak in hushed tones about the mother who routinely takes time out to do things for herself. The 'self-sacrificing mother' is idolized and revered in cultures and across the world, even as she falls apart herself, while the one who ensures that she also takes care of her own needs is branded as a 'selfish mother'.

I am fairly convinced that the airline safety announcement, 'Please ensure that you put on your own oxygen mask before assisting others,' was introduced after an incident with a mother travelling with her kids. I can picture her lying on the floor of the plane gasping for breath and imploring a co-passenger for help, not with her own mask but with the mask of one of her children.

For most mothers (and fathers), their contentment lies in the happiness of the children. We become 'moms' first and everything else later. We want that halo of being a 'good mother' to our kids so much that we neglect and even bury our own needs and desires.

But sooner or later, the cracks start to appear. It took several years and many cracks for me to realize that focusing on myself, at times, and making decisions that were optimal for me, when necessary, did not make me a 'bad mother'. In fact, those moments of focus on myself may even help make me a better parent.

There is a scene in the movie *Date Night* when Tina Fey's character tells her husband about her deepest fantasy. Her husband, a typical man, assumes that it is a sexual fantasy and waits with baited breath for her to describe it. What she says next would resonate with every mother.

'There are times when I've just thought about, on my worst day, just, you know, leaving our house and going some place. Like checking into a hotel and just being in a quiet room by myself. Just sitting in a quiet, air-conditioned room, sitting down, eating my lunch with no one touching me, drinking a Diet Sprite, by myself.'

Rings true, doesn't it?

I too have had moments when I have briefly fantasized about running away for a weekend. Escaping to a place where I would have some peace, quiet and alone time for two days.

A child would not be tugging at my trouser leg. Another

child would not be asking me to find a missing book or piece of a puzzle. I would not be stepping over broken toys and yelling at one of the kids to finish their homework while trying to convince another to take a bath.

Running away without a forwarding address or phone number, just for a few days, is my deepest, darkest fantasy.

Does that make me selfish? Perhaps, it does.

I wouldn't give up or trade the many moments of joy that I have had spending time with my children. I love them immensely and am extremely grateful for them. But I can't deny it—there is a piece of me that sometimes misses 'me'.

35: I Hate You, Mommy!

He stood in the doorway of the room. His fists were tightly clenched by his side, his eyes were puffy and red from crying and I could see the nerve in his neck pulsing as he drew in short, sharp breaths.

He looked at me in anger and screamed, 'I hate you! I wish I wasn't your child. I wish you would just go away!'

I remember exactly where I was standing at that moment, no more than five feet away from my extremely emotional seven-year-old son in the living-room of our apartment. And I remember how badly his words stung. It felt like someone had punched me in the stomach and knocked the air out of me. How could he say something like that to me? Barely a half hour ago, we were sitting together talking about his school day and laughing at the stories from the playground that he was sharing with me.

How did things go so wrong, so soon?

He had asked if he could have a play date with a close friend the next day. He had already spoken with his friend and they both thought that it was a good idea. His friend's mother had given her consent for it too. But we had other plans for the next day, and I had put a spanner in the works by asking the boys to wait for the following week.

To my young son, this was nothing short of apocalyptic. I was a little annoyed by his initial reaction of stomping his feet and insisting that he have his play date the next day. I recognized that he was going to have a tantrum over the issue. I told him firmly that there would be no play date the next day and if he didn't behave himself soon, there would be none the next week either.

He stormed off angrily into his room. He had had tantrums before and he usually needed to be left alone for a few minutes to cool down and get back to his usual happy self. After that, we would typically have a small chat about what was the appropriate behaviour to express his views and thoughts.

I decided to leave him alone until he had calmed down. Less than ten minutes later, he emerged from his room. But, instead of looking like he had calmed down, he seemed even more upset.

I started to walk towards him, arms outstretched to hold him. No mother likes to see her child upset and I knew that my son was still at the age when hugs were exactly what were needed to soothe frayed nerves.

But I was stopped by his scream. 'I hate you! I wish I wasn't your child. I wish you would just go away!'

I was stunned. He had been upset with me before, but *hate*? My arms fell to my sides.

'You don't mean that,' I replied, in as calm a voice as I could muster, although I could feel myself quivering.

'I do! I do hate you! You're the worst!'

He spun around and went back into his room, slamming the door.

I felt the sting in my eyes as the tears welled up. Did

he mean it? Did my adorable little boy, who along with his brother and sister, was the most precious being in the universe for me, really hate me?

He had had tantrums earlier. He had thrown himself on the floor when denied something he had wanted, kicked his feet and flailed his arms while crying bitterly. So I had seen emotional outbursts previously from my son. But he had never said he *hated* me.

I wondered if I had been too harsh on him. Had I pushed him over the edge for him to feel this way? Could I have handled the situation better? Should I change my mind, allow him to have that play date and somehow figure out the logistics for the day? Obviously, it meant so much to him.

But if I didn't stand my ground, would he ever take anything I said in the future seriously? Would every parenting decision I took be up for negotiation?

I peeked into his room. He was lying on his bed, staring out of the window. He noticed me at the door and turned his head in the other direction, without saying a word.

I walked up to the bed and sat down on it. I could sense him tensing up. I put a hand gently on his leg. Tears started to stream down his face and mine.

'I love you, baby. And I'll love you forever, no matter how you feel about me,' I told him. 'And I am so happy that you are my child.'

His tears kept flowing but he didn't say a word. I told him that I was sorry that he felt the way he did, but he had to understand that I made some decisions based on what was best for all of us as a family. He would get to have his play date next week, but he would have to be patient for now.

There was no response from him. I patted his leg for a

little longer and then got up and left his room. A few minutes later, he came out of his room, walked over to the couch where I was and sat down next to me. I put my arm around him and he buried his head in my shoulders. More tears were shed as he told me that he loved me and didn't mean what he had said earlier. I held him close and told him that it was okay and that I loved him.

That was the first time I heard my child saying, 'I hate you'. Unfortunately, it hasn't been the last. I've heard it over a dozen times over the last few years as my son has approached and entered the adolescence period. In recent times, he hasn't been that quick to recant it either, and the sulking period often goes on for much longer.

At times, I've been angry when he has said that to me. I've wanted to retort with something hurtful of my own like, 'You ungrateful twit, you have no idea what I have done for you!' But then I've reminded myself that in any parent-child argument, it is best for at least one person, ideally the parent, to remain *reasonably* mature.

I know from other mothers that they too have heard this dreaded phrase from their children. In many instances, it has been said because the children want to exert their influence on a decision. Sometimes, they've said it to get a reaction from their parents.

I know my son doesn't mean it. I know he says it in the heat of the moment and I know that a few hours later, it will all be forgotten.

It still hurts, but not nearly as badly as it did when I first heard it from him.

Most importantly, I hope he knows that no matter how he feels, his mother will always love him just the same. She may cancel a few play dates, embarrass him in front of his school buddies and bother him to complete his homework, but she'll always adore him.

And I hope that one day, while I am in earshot, his young child also tells him that he/she hates him. Payback from future generations is a mother's best revenge!

36: Missing the Embrace

It began with subtle signs in third grade.

Up until second grade, my oldest son wanted me to drop him off at the entrance of his classroom, and would happily accept and return my hugs and kisses in full view of all his classmates. As he walked towards his seat, he would look back and wave goodbye to me with flying kisses and a big grin.

That was always the best part of my morning. The hugs that I got from my children when I dropped them off to their classrooms were my battery pack. They charged me up and powered by them, I was ready to take on the day. Our goodbye hugs and kisses lasted only a few seconds but their effect stayed on for several hours.

In third grade, my son began to turn around to face me outside the classroom, and said goodbye rather unceremoniously.

No hugs, no kisses. Just a simple, 'Goodbye, Mom. See you later.'

When I tried to pull him into an embrace, he pushed me away abruptly and whispered in a sharp voice, 'Stop embarrassing me! My friends are watching.'

He then walked straight into the classroom and joined

a group of his friends in their conversation. He didn't look back even once to see if I was still there or to wave goodbye.

Talk about betrayal.

I felt rejected. Those goodbye hugs and kisses had made me feel wanted in my son's life. They were a tangible connection between us and meant a lot. Probably, as I realized then, they meant much more to me than they did to him.

I was heartbroken at the rejection. Unhugged and feeling rather unloved, I trudged away slowly from the classroom door.

My oldest son was no longer 'mummy's boy'.

Not in public, at least.

At home, he was only too happy to sit in my lap, cuddle with me on the couch and be smothered with my kisses. But in school, his 'coolness quotient' was severely hampered by any interaction of less than an arm's-length distance with me.

By the time he reached fifth grade, I was no longer wanted on the same floor in school. My mere presence in the vicinity of his classroom was enough for him to be terrified that his friends would sneer at him for having 'Mommy' around.

Fortunately, with the two younger ones, I was still getting hugs outside *their* classrooms, but now I was painfully aware that the clock was ticking on those too. Perhaps it was a growing insecurity and my runaway imagination, but I began to stress that even their hugs were getting a little less tight. Instead of holding on to me until their teacher called them into the classroom, they were disengaging a bit too quickly. They were hugging me, but their attention had already moved towards their friends. It was a reminder for me to enjoy those moments while they lasted. I had already painfully witnessed their disappearance with one child.

Now that he is in middle school, my oldest is dropped off

at the curb. I am neither required nor invited by him to enter the building. Going by early indicators of behaviour, I suspect that a similar pattern will follow with his younger siblings. I have started looking for other sources of energy and power in the morning, such as double espressos.

Given my impact on their 'coolness quotient', I will be saddened, but not surprised, if my children tell me not to come within a hundred metres of the school perimeter once they reach high school.

I'll just make a note to remind them of that when they bring home their dirty laundry from college.

37: Are You a Tiger Mom?

A fellow mom asked me if I was a tiger mother. I had to think about it for a while.

I wasn't sure.

My Indian background does give me a natural propensity to be one. In an environment where there are a limited number of seats in pre-schools, and even more limited spots in regular schools, with intense competition for each one, becoming a tiger mom often becomes a rite of passage before the child turns five.

In fact, in India, being called a tiger mom can be seen as a compliment. It implies that you are completely involved in your child's development and progress and keenly aware of what they need to do in academics, sports and extra-curricular activities to position themselves for success. In Indian society, the scholastic and extra-curricular achievements of children often determine the social worth of the parents. As a result, a parenting approach that involves hovering over and even smothering your child with opinions and instructions is viewed by many as favourable and even necessary.

But being a tiger mom (or dad, sometimes) is not easy.

I have seen mothers sitting for hours outside squash courts

pointing out flaws in techniques or strategy to their sons or daughters. I have heard of fathers working with their children in swimming pools at the crack of dawn to refine their strokes. I have known of instances where parents have stayed up late making a copious amount of study notes for their children, so that they can understand and remember the material better.

I have tried hard to be a tiger mom as well. On some occasions, this is how the afternoon progresses in my home:

> Me (to older son): Have you done your homework yet?
> Older son: (sprawled on the couch in front of TV) I just got home. Can I get fifteen minutes, please?
> (Twenty minutes of pacing later.)
> Me: How about starting that homework now?
> Older son: I'll start it after this episode finishes.
> Me: Get up and do your homework now!
> Older son: (storming off into his room) You're always yelling at me! Fine, I'm doing it!

I turn my attention to my second son, who is still struggling to finish his post-school snack.

> Me: Have you practised on the keyboard?
> Second son: (playing with the snack on his plate) I practised last week.
> Me: Are you trying to be funny? Get up and practise on the keyboard now!
> Second son: (storming off) You're always shouting at me!

Having sorted out the afternoon for two of my children, I turn to my youngest child, who is yet again arranging her dolls on the bed.

Me: Have you read a book today?
Daughter: I'm playing with my dolls.
Me: I can see that. I asked you if you had read a book.
Daughter: I'm playing with my dolls.
At this point, I am wondering if I need to take all three kids to the doctor for a hearing examination.
Me: Bring a book to me now and let me hear you read it out aloud.
Daughter: (stomping her feet) You're always scolding me!
Me: (in my firmest voice) Book. Read. Now.
My daughter brings a book over while holding a doll in her hand. I yank the doll out and make her sit in the chair next to me.
Me: Ok. Start reading.
Daughter (haltingly): A long time ago, the kildren of a vi-vill...
Me: It's not 'kildren', it's 'children'. I told you that when the letters c and h are together, they make a 'ch' sound.
Daughter: Oh. The children of a vill-villa-villag...
Me: It's 'vill-age'. Come on. Try harder. This time, try it in English.
Daughter: I was reading in English!
Me: (under my breath) You had me fooled.
Daughter: What?
Me: Sorry. Please continue.

Now, I realize that I may be too harsh on my children. But in an increasingly competitive world where three-year-old music prodigies and six-year-old computer geniuses are routinely showcased, your type-A personality along with its several insecurities comes to the surface. You push your child because you feel the pressure more than them. Their performance, after all, is a reflection of the kind of job you are doing as their parent.

After we finally (and painfully) finish six pages of the book, it is clear that we both need a break. I decide to take a look at how my oldest child is progressing in his homework and peek into his room.

> Me: How's the homework coming along?
> Older son: Fine. I'm doing my math homework right now.
> Me: Can I help you with any of it?
> Older son: Yes. I'm confused by a question that asks what happens when -5 is multiplied by -4.
> Me: Simple, the answer is twenty. Why is that difficult?
> Older son: But why is it that a negative number multiplied by another negative number results in a positive number? Why isn't it -20? It just doesn't make sense to me.
> Me: (slightly flummoxed because I don't know why either, but I can't admit that to him) Don't ask silly questions. It just does.
> Older son: (shrugs his shoulders) Ok. Can you help me understand how to find the greatest common factor between 24 and 64?
> Me: Well, you would find the prime factors of both the numbers, then multiply those in common and you would have your answer.
> Older son: Huh?
> Me: (annoyed) Hasn't your teacher taught this to you in class?

> Older son: She did, but I didn't fully understand it and your explanation is even more confusing.
> Me: (completely exasperated) Well, if you paid more attention in class, we wouldn't be struggling with this right now! Just take the common prime factors and multiply them. Now, do you have any other questions?
> Older son: (hesitantly) No. I think I'll be fine on my own.
> Me: Good. I want to see an A in this class.

Now that I had ensured my older son understood his math homework well, I wanted to make sure my second son was being diligent with his work on the keyboard. I entered the room where he was practising and sat down next to him.

> Me: How is the practice coming along?
> Second son: I can't understand some of the instructions that my teacher has left for me on the practice sheet.
> Me: Can I help you?
> Second son: I don't understand how to change the key signature of this piece into a minor. And then, I need to play it in a *ritardando* tempo and it's challenging to do that consistently.
> Me: Huh? Does anyone in this house speak English anymore?

So maybe this was a particularly trying day in our household, but the fact of the matter is that being a tiger mom is not easy. It requires a tremendous amount of self-discipline, dedication and hard work.

The shouting at the kids is the easy part. The harder part is to learn the theory of music myself to be able to work with my younger son on it, or understand how to explain phonetics to my daughter as she learns to read.

Being a successful tiger mom means having the patience to explain the underlying concepts of numbers and their operations in math to your child. It means having the discipline to sit with your child while they slowly (and painfully) practise their piano pieces on a regular basis. It means having the openness to learn new ways of teaching your child by unlearning what you know and then relearning it so you can coach them.

It means being ready to put your life on hold while you accompany your child to 6.00 a.m. swim lessons or out of town training programmes. It means giving up on many of your aspirations in order to support your child in chasing their dreams.

I've tried to be a tiger mom on some occasions. It has not been easy, and it hasn't always borne the best results for either my children or me.

It's a lot of work. And I have the utmost respect for mothers and fathers who can be these tiger parents.

But I have also seen some of them take it too far. I am thinking of the mother who yelled at her daughter after a 5,000-metre swim for finishing three seconds behind another girl. The poor, exhausted child just swam five kilometres! I am sure a pat on the back and a banana would have been more appropriate and welcome. I am also thinking of the father who wouldn't speak to his child after he lost a squash match. The young boy needed a pep talk to get his spirits back up, not the cold treatment.

I have seen some kids revolt against their tiger parents by refusing to go to athletic tournaments, music recitals or even school, because of the inordinate amount of pressure that has been placed on them.

I faced some of that too, when my oldest son decided that he wouldn't be playing any more squash tournaments because he didn't like the look on my face when he lost. It was a lesson to me to be careful about the emotions that I was expressing and transferring to him.

I think each one of us has to find our equilibrium with our children. What works for me with one child doesn't work with another. One of my children is much more laid back than his/her siblings and performs at their best when relaxed. Pushing that child further doesn't result in a positive outcome, and I've learned to back off and let this one take charge of what they need to do with minimal guidance and oversight.

Another child needs constant goading, which often causes strife between us. But both of us also know that at least for now, that's the only way to get him to near his potential.

Sometimes, rather than tiger moms, our kids need cheerleaders. And they need those cheerleaders most when they aren't doing as well as they would like to. I'm not suggesting showering them with empty praise when they come home with a less than satisfactory test result. The Indian mother in me would never allow that. But I do think we need to appreciate their hard work and sincere effort. When my son loses a closely fought five-set match, I want to be there to cheer him on and take him out for a treat. When my daughter finishes reading her book by herself, even if takes her twice as long as it should, I want to give her a high-five. When my child yells in frustration at not being able to complete a piano piece flawlessly even after hours of trying, I want to give him a pat on the back and ask him to try again the next day.

That's not easy either. My inner competitive parent wants them to shine in everything in which they are involved. I want them to excel academically, and I want them to perform well in their other activities.

But then, I have to remind myself that this is just the start of a long journey for them. I could push them on something now, but at what cost? It could dent their self-confidence, their pursuit of the activity in the longer term, and even their relationship with me. Is that a price I am willing to pay for near-term success?

Striking the right balance and positively motivating the children to perform to the best of their abilities is what parents seek to do. We don't always succeed. Sometimes, we fall short. Sometimes, we overcompensate. But as parents, our job is to keep trying. Because, as much as the kids need to learn, so do we.

Epilogue

Being a parent is a tough job. An incredibly difficult job with zero training, negligible feedback and few opportunities to get a second chance.

There is no high school or college course that teaches you how to be a good parent. There isn't any online curriculum which can be followed to gain insights on becoming an effective parent. There isn't even a standardized test that predicts the probability of your success in that role before you plunge head-first into it.

There are no apprenticeships or internships for you to get an understanding of what the job entails. And there is no 'easing in' period either. You are simply thrown into the deep end with a newborn in your arms.

The stakes are high and you are paranoid about making mistakes along the way. Unfortunately, there's very little by way of performance evaluation that you get in the initial years. So you wonder, or rather obsess, about how you are faring.

There are many nights when I go to bed wondering if I did right by my kids. And sometimes, that answer is *no*.

I could have been more patient. I could have been more understanding. I could have spent a little more time listening and a little less time sermonizing.

I could have made sure they ate their five servings of fruit and vegetables.

(Perhaps if I weren't eating a burger myself, it would have been easier to convince them.)

I could have raised my voice less. I could have hugged more.

Instead of just talking to my children about the values that I wanted them to grow up with, I could have demonstrated the same values through my actions.

I could have folded the newspaper or put away my mobile phone when my child came and sat next to me. I could have turned and faced her and gently stroked her hair while she told me the stories of her dolls for the seventeenth time.

I could have taken my kids to the park to run around instead of turning on the television to get them to sit quietly in one place.

I could have read another book to my daughter instead of fussing over how late it was getting. I could have held my son a little longer as he fell asleep.

I could have done a lot of things differently.

But when I see the smiles on my children's faces and the sparkle in their eyes, I also know that I did, at least, a few things well.

I know I won't get each day right. I am fairly certain that I will never get any day to be perfect. But as long as we've got enough good days, we should be fine.

I hope.